T0199119

FAMILY SKELETONS

FAMILY SKELETONS

A Web of Mental Illness

ELAYNE GILLIAM

FAMILY SKELETONS
A WEB OF MENTAL ILLNESS

iUniverse books may be ordered through booksellers or by contacting:

iUniverse
1663 Liberty Drive
Bloomington, IN 47403
www.iuniverse.com
1-800-Authors (1-800-288-4677)

Autobiography
All names have been changed

ISBN: 978-1-5320-6072-4 (sc)
ISBN: 978-1-5320-6073-1 (e)

Library of Congress Control Number: 2018913398

Print information available on the last page.

iUniverse rev. date: 11/09/2018

In memory of my eldest daughter:
with gratitude for the years I
enjoyed as your mother and
sorrow that I was unable to save you.

CONTENTS

Prologue: A Cry for Help ix

1   Friday the Thirteenth 1
2   Early Challenges 9
3   A New Beginning 19
4   Falling Through the Cracks 29
5   Out of the Woodwork 37
6   Dora's Struggles 41
7   There's Been a Tragedy 47
8   Saying Goodbye 57
9   Letting Go 63
10   Guns 69
11   A Visit With Bret 73
12   My Closet 77
13   Skeletons 83
14   Bret Missing 93
15   The Graveyard Revisited 99

Appendices 103
Reviews 111
Book Blurb 113
About The Author 115

PROLOGUE
A Cry for Help

A small rural police station in the Sierra Nevada was experiencing a typical quiet day when the switchboard received an emergency call concerning a woman alone in a local cemetery. Two officers quickly climbed into a patrol car and headed up the narrow main road toward the remote graveyard. Past the outskirts of town, they followed a winding dirt road until they entered a small, unkempt, nineteenth-century cemetery on the edge of a canyon. At the site, they saw an abandoned car adjacent to the dilapidated, weed-covered wooden fence surrounding the old burial ground. Exiting their vehicle, the officers cautiously approached a small figure kneeling among some new graves.

Surrounding her were old weathered stones that testified to a long history. Many carried only the word *unknown*, with a reference to the past when gold miners tramped through the area and sometimes died alone. The rundown cemetery also chronicled the deaths of whole families of children, such as the "Five Little Neals," likely wiped out during epidemics in the late 1800s. Today, despite the site's isolation, it remained a choice burial site for some residents.

Cautiously, the officers approached the woman who was slumped with her back to them. The first officer got close and assessed the situation before asking her to give him the knife she held. With the article secured, he asked questions, trying to judge her mental condition. As the other officer moved near her, she said, "You are standing on my husband's grave." Embarrassed, he moved toward the next site, and she again complained, "You are on my other husband's and my daughter's graves." After further dialogue, one officer asked the woman to consent to be driven to the local hospital. Condescendingly, she slowly rose and followed the officers through the rugged, rocky terrain to their patrol car, leaving her vehicle abandoned.

In silence, they started the slow descent through the worn, single-lane roads to the main street. On the way, they stopped at the local fire station where emergency volunteers had assembled. Assured that all was under control, they started the drive to the psychiatric care facility. The only conversation during this trip was from the officer who asked, "Do you know what you have done?" Perhaps he was referring to the time and manpower taken to reach her, suggesting that he was not sympathetic. The woman remained silent, engaged in her own thoughts. She had brought no personal belongings, and her car remained abandoned. What was she thinking?

Upon reaching the hospital, she was taken through locked doors and remanded to a nurse. A physician, whom she obviously recognized, was waiting. Following admission, she requested that her younger military son be advised of her situation, but she neglected to advise anyone that she had left a mentally disabled son alone at her home. During a week of observation, she remained docile and quietly complied with her treatment. A few relatives and one gentleman, who claimed to be related, visited her briefly and found her confused and withdrawn. Meanwhile, friends retrieved her car from the cemetery and returned it to her home but did not talk to her ill son.

Following her evaluation, it was apparent that the woman had cried out for help. Records revealed that years earlier she had endured the loss of her first husband, the father of her children, to Lou Gehrig's disease. Recently she had buried another husband following twenty years of marriage, during which time she saw him through heart surgeries and cancer. Two years following his death, her eldest daughter committed suicide with a gun. The woman was the primary caregiver for a paranoid schizophrenic son and recently had been diagnosed with post-traumatic stress disorder. Although friends had tried to help her, she felt overwhelmed with grief. She had found that her son's dual diagnosis of alcoholism and mental illness, along with the public misunderstanding of these conditions, intolerable to cope with.

This is more than a random woman's story; it relates a family saga of struggles with alcoholism and mental illness in various forms. It begins with me, the author, sharing my life as a naive young woman with hopes for a long, happy marriage and family. Was it an omen that my first child was born on Friday the thirteenth? The story begins with great expectations in rural New Hampshire and eventually continues in Northern California, where I was left widowed with four children and few skills to support my family. I write looking back on a life that covers nearly ninety years, still with an ability to laugh, to joke, and to entertain others with my stories. Few of my friends are aware of the tragedies behind my seemingly jovial image. I have developed a persona that belies a past of abuse and struggle. After years of keeping journals about my experiences with family mental illness, I have endeavored to share them in the hope of benefiting others.

From California to Virginia, and finally to Myrtle Beach, South Carolina, I look back on tragedy and hope, four marriages, and the success of my two younger children. Here I finally share some conclusions about my own fights with mental illness. As the struggle continues with loss and hope, I find it hard to accept that the mental illness my family and I have known and continue to bear is a battle we alone contend with. Hopefully others will find things they share in my revelations, and my secrets may help others to move on as I have. My inspiration for this work came from a discarded book I retrieved at a garage sale. In it a mother, the wife of a doctor, shared her story of life with a mentally ill son who became a stranger to her. I realized then that I was not alone and that I must also share my story.

1

Friday the Thirteenth

It was Friday the thirteenth, and the birth of our first child was now one week overdue. An obstetrical nurse had arrived seven days earlier and had spent time entertaining me while preparing for my home delivery. One day, in hopes of starting my labor, she suggested a car ride over some rough country roads. Soon, as we drove through the local countryside, I tried to ignore the onset of discomfort. It was August, and summer was in its warmest and most pleasant season of the year, which for me was always too brief in New England. I thought about how soon September would arrive with a chill and that I would need to prepare for winter while taking care of a new baby. The recent move to New Hampshire, a day trip away from my parents, had seemed idyllic to me. I could admit to myself that I had married to get away from my mother. It seemed perfect, and I basked in the independence I was enjoying. I wrote to friends that since getting married I had learned to cook, paint and wallpaper the apartment, make draperies, upholster, and decorate. However, here I was, without family, facing childbirth, which was an experience I had forgotten to include in my love of freedom from my mother.

As we continued driving, my back was suddenly enveloped in rhythmic pain, and I was relieved when we finally returned to our small home. We climbed the stairs to the second floor of the old Victorian-style house, with its view of a chicken yard next door and a few cows beyond in a pasture. Across the street was a new hospital that I had not opted to use for my first delivery. It was a decision made more from fear of hospitals and the smells of medicine than of concern about the birth process. I was content to be in my own pleasant environment and had never discussed my decision to have a home birth with my mother.

With labor pains increasing, the nurse became aware of my condition and sprang into action. First she delegated my husband to telephone duty. It was early evening, and he had difficulty locating the doctor, ironically named Dr. Blood, who we learned was in his pasture gathering his cows. As I paced the floor, an assistant doctor arrived to assess my progress. "It might be midnight," he concluded. Then he left for his birthday celebration, assured that I had some hours of labor ahead. As my contractions quickly progressed, I sensed the nurse was tense with the prospect that she might be delivering a mother's first baby alone. While still standing, I leaned on her shoulder until she asked me to get on the bed. The only information my mother had given me about childbirth was "Just sneeze hard." That advice did not work well as huge contractions wracked my abdomen.

During my pregnancy, I had studied two books about baby care, one by Dr. Spock and the other by Better Homes and Gardens, but I had thought little of the impending experience of childbirth, especially a home birth. The first trimester of my pregnancy had been difficult, as I endured severe morning sickness. I had seen my obstetrician periodically and had been dismissed casually with the understanding that he would deliver my baby at home. He finally arrived at nine o'clock, just in time to help the anxious nurse deliver a large baby boy without complications. There was excitement over his safe arrival, his mop of dark hair, and his hearty wails.

After making phone calls to my parents, my husband and I basked in the thrill of having a healthy son. We were unable to foresee the future and the problems that would confront our life. Growing up, our son would refer to his birth on Friday the thirteenth as an omen and an excuse for his later disability. "But," I reminded him then, "the doctor who first came to deliver you was also born on Friday the thirteenth."

In retrospect, it might seem odd that I had not shared the news of my pregnancy with my parents for four months. My husband and I had visited their country home for Thanksgiving when I first suspected I was pregnant, but I had said nothing. We were a private family that shared little conversation and had been taught to "be seen and not heard." I wondered if this admonition was from my father's little English mother. I had sought no advice from my mother on birthing, and she had spoken little of her experiences having five children. Our recent move to a small town, some distance from my parents, allowed me the privacy regarding my condition. Following weeks of severe morning sickness, I worked as a receptionist a few months, and for this I had sewn my own maternity wardrobe. Halfway through my pregnancy, we decided to visit my parents' country home when I announced the pregnancy. My news was soon upstaged by the discovery that my youngest brother and his high school girlfriend were also expecting. Eventually they had a baby boy, born six weeks after my son's birth.

During this trip, I recalled that while in high school I had contracted the mumps, and my mother chose that time, when I was confined, to discuss some intimate things about marriage and babies to me. She had asked me to join her in the kitchen where she had set up a card table for us to play rummy. Soon, however, the game time turned into a quiz of my knowledge about life and sex. First I recall being asked if I knew where babies came from, and I answered, half bored, that I did not. My life then consisted of dreams of being a ballerina or an artist. I had never owned pets, and the question of reproduction had not concerned me. Awkwardly, Mother tried to engage me in further conversation about the facts of life. As she continued her questioning, I became more uncomfortable, but she insisted on trying to find out if I knew anything. She couldn't fathom that I simply had never thought about how babies get here. The subject had simply not concerned me, even when she had become pregnant and had my sister when I was fifteen. I was too involved in activities outside of our home to pay any attention to my mother's condition. After all, she had spent most of her pregnancy in bed.

Our home life was devoid of conversation, and we never dared to ask questions of our parents. When we approached our father about problems, we were told not to bother him. What little I knew about life I learned from my girlfriends. Meanwhile, the rummy game ended with me in tears and my mother totally confused and distraught. I think I was overwhelmed by my mother's first attempt in my life to have a conversation with me.

Soon after the birth of our son, my parents visited us to welcome their first grandchild. My father was reluctant to hold the infant, but my mother relished the new role of grandmother. She commented on how painful childbirth was and pointed out that my stomach was still enlarged. My mother had an obsession about the size of a woman's stomach. It was either flat like hers or fat, which to her was unacceptable. I thought, *We all carry excess weight somewhere*. Hers was on her fanny and mine on my stomach. Since I had recently delivered an eight-pound baby, I thought it normal that I would not have my figure back yet.

This criticism reminded me of an incident when I was fifteen. One day, I confronted my father in the hallway at home, and he looked at me and commented, "Don't gain any more weight." At the time, I had suddenly gone through a weight gain during puberty from less than one hundred pounds to one hundred thirteen. Next, my mother took me to a doctor where she complained that I had a large stomach. Without any testing, the doctor advised that I was a normal weight for my age and dismissed us. Indignant, my mother took me to the nearest department store and purchased a girdle that I was obliged to wear until I grew independent enough to choose to wear pantyhose.

It was no wonder that throughout my life I was sensitive about my weight, which luckily varied little from my teen years. Luckily, I had inherited the physique of my little English grandmother.

Meanwhile, following my parents' visit, I resorted to the help of Dr. Spock's book as our son, I will call him Bret, grew fast. What I had not read anywhere was that my baby would gain too much weight drinking the milk from a local farm with cream so rich on top that I could easily whip it. However, once he started running and climbing, he slimmed down. As Bret grew, he enjoyed watching me cook and would climb on a stool to try to help. His interests also extended to pulling out drawers that then toppled dressers. Throughout his childhood, he had the disconcerting habit of waking early, about five o'clock. He never allowed us the luxury of sleeping in, and he continued this habit throughout his life. Later, when Bret was a toddler, we once awakened to find he had climbed out of his crib and disappeared. After notifying the police, he was found wandering down the street from the house.

Since my marriage, my mother had allowed my young sister to stay alone with us, or sometimes they would show up together. On one occasion, we planned a picnic with neighbors in a wooded area where my husband worked as a gardener. As we hiked across the lawns to the picnic tables, my mother suddenly ran ahead of us and threw herself rolling down a hill. I guess we all have those moments when we wish we could forget our inhibitions and partake of our childhood fun. However, the unexpected act of my mother tumbling down a hill in her nice skirt and blouse was embarrassing. I attributed some of my mother's unpredictable behavior to her uninhibited personality. She had lived through the wild flapper years and felt free of tradition. My parents often laughed about escapades that they and business friends engaged in, such as sliding down the banister of the Waldorf Astoria in New York City. Mother usually talked with a cigarette in the corner of her mouth, spewing ashes, with hands on her hips. In contrast, girls of my generation were expected to behave like Princess Elizabeth.

During the Depression, my parents and their friends had created their own entertainment. When I was growing up, our home was the scene of frequent parties with a conga line circling through the downstairs rooms and plenty of drink and laughter. My mother played the piano and a friend, the violin. There were contrasting standards set for my generation: the gloves, the hat with a veil when we went to church, and that uncomfortable girdle. By this time in my life, bones in the girdle had pressed so long against my ribs that a large cyst had formed on my abdomen; it required surgery with seven stitches. I had a hard time explaining the scar to doctors the rest of my life. It was following the delivery of my son that I again resorted to the girdle in hopes of regaining my youthful figure.

Visits from my mother and sister were not always harmonious. When we had my sister alone, my husband bought her books to read, which she remembers with fondness. However, one long visit with my sister and my mother erupted into a loud argument. Often Mother would think of a contentious subject that she would mull over and then insist that I agree with. When I expressed disagreement, she became upset and pouted, or she turned on me for not confirming her opinions. On one occasion, I refused to agree with a disparaging remark she made about one of my three brothers. I knew that if I agreed, she would then gossip saying the subject originated with me. The brother in question had always been the object of my mother's abuse. I thought he was handsome, but for some unknown reason, she always took her wrath out on him. Over the years, he responded by letting everything go in one ear and out the other. He developed a defense mechanism that he later used with all of us.

As Mother continued her ranting, I became increasingly upset to the point where we were shouting. Finally she decided to leave abruptly with my sister in hand and drive to her mother's house, where she would find a sympathetic listener. For three days following this episode, I feared I was having a heart attack. I could hardly breathe, and I suffered fierce stress. This episode changed the relationship with my mother forever. From that time on, I was wary of talking with her. Although her habit of imposing her beliefs on me continued, it resulted with my complete distrust of her. I realized that friendships with any of my three sisters-in-law were contaminated by my mother's version of facts, which she insisted they were. My marriage and those of my siblings eventually ended in divorce, and contacts with former spouses were not frequent. Meanwhile, as a result of disputes with my mother, my distrust of everyone hampered relationships throughout my life. I often felt lonely and unable to confide in or trust others, especially women, while still longing to have closer relationships with them. Earlier in my life, I had been diagnosed by elders as someone always looking for a mother. My friends were usually my parents' age. And as I grew older, my friendships were often with women my daughters' age rather than my own. For the remainder of my life, Mother rarely visited me, and the subject of my weight never came up again because I remained thin.

Following four pleasant years in the small town, my husband accepted a job in Connecticut where we settled into a home on the campus of a private school. Soon after moving, we anticipated the birth of our second child. Fortunately, I planned a home birth again because this baby allowed me no time to spare once I started labor. A friend had just had a home birth and offered me the services of her nurse. She had no sooner arrived than she asked me to climb onto the four-poster bed after which my water immediately broke. The doctor, who was savoring a cup of coffee in the living room, ran in when my delivery was suddenly over. Without a pain, I had a healthy baby girl. It was early morning, June 21. With the speed of the birth, I realized that I could never have made it to a hospital. Even the attending doctor seemed surprised and relieved at the suddenness of the delivery.

Now my husband and I dreamed of a happy life with a healthy son and a beautiful daughter, whom I named after my little English grandmother. Our lives at that time remained uneventful as we enjoyed and adored the children. Our son, Bret, delighted in the fireflies that swarmed about the house at night. He called them "light bangs."

On campus, Bret attended a nursery school where there were complaints that he was teasing other children. At home, he never showed this tendency and got along well with his baby sister. We detected nothing abnormal with the children other than slow speech development. I wondered if it was difficult for them to understand their father's deep, quiet voice. And my life in a family where little conversation was allowed did not prepare me to encourage talking with my children. I did love to rock my children, and as they grew, I played with them on the floor, and lying on my back, I raised them high above me with my legs. I remember the day, all too soon, when my youngest child no longer allowed me to rock her. How I missed holding a child in my lap, and I had to wait many years for grandchildren to fall asleep as I rocked them. Raising children had many precious moments, such as playing cards on the floor, pulling a sled, dressing Barbie dolls, and reading nursery rhyme books. The girls collected toy horses, and the boys played drums. My biggest regret was my inability to converse, to talk more, and all because of my own childhood with little conversation.

After four memorable and happy years at his job, my husband again decided to move, this time to the West Coast. I rarely had seen my parents during this period, so I had missed much of the adolescent growth spurt of my young sister, whom I barely recognized on an infrequent visit. We had usually spent our holidays alone or with friends and never took the children on the four-hour visit to my parents' home. By this time, my brothers had all married and settled where they could get jobs, and our lives never crossed. I felt a sense of peace in the role of wife and mother, and I was especially happy separated from my mother. The decision to move meant that I was never again to live in my native and picturesque New England; I only returned once for my fifty-fifth high school class reunion. By then I had been widowed twice, our daughter Dora was ill, and Bret was suffering from mental illness. It was on that last trip that I saw an elderly uncle, the only relative who ever expressed concern about my personality growing up. He spoke of me once as "a wounded bird." I had come a long way since childhood, and I delighted in taking him to lunch and sharing my success in overcoming what seemed like a challenging childhood.

2

Early Challenges

The decision to move west, of course, was my husband's. Perhaps he missed his family, which by now had migrated from a small town in British Columbia to California, which he chose as our next place to settle. We planned to cross the country with two children and all of our belongings in a new Dodge and a truck he purchased for $400. On a Sunday, we packed everything and started out for what was to be a long night's trip to my parents' home. Throughout the trip, Dora slept on the back seat of the car while my husband led the way in the truck with Bret seated at his side. About halfway along the Pennsylvania Turnpike, the truck engine caught fire. With a quick stop on the side of the highway, my husband grabbed our son's winter jacket, opened the truck hood, and smothered the fire. For years, memories of this haunted me. The truck could have blown up while our son slept on the front seat. Shaken and short of sleep, we reached our destination, and we recuperated at my parents' home for a week before continuing the move.

During the visit, I met my middle brother's new wife and sang at their wedding. Before we left, my father asked another brother to find out how much money we had for the trip. Dad then added another one hundred dollars to our meager funds, which were later desperately needed. It was during this trip that my sister, now an adolescent, spoke to me about a mysterious phone call she had answered. "Dad turned pale when he took the call," she related, describing the voice as that of a young boy. Our dad had become angry and admonished the caller, saying, "I thought I told you never to call this number." This evoked a memory from my childhood when I found my mother in her room crying. I asked her what was wrong, and she replied, "I'm not happy." I returned to the front porch where I found my father sitting dejected and distant in a rocker. I then recalled rumors of my father having an affair.

A previous incident that I thought was curious at the time, and perhaps related, was when our father assembled us at an attorney's office to sign some papers. At the time, we were informed that along with the five of us there was another unknown person added to the signatures. My mother nervously dismissed the mystery saying a boy in a wheelchair was included. Not until my father's funeral did I learn that my father did indeed have another child, born out of wedlock when I was about eight years old. His mother, I learned, was a dancer whose picture Dad kept in his dresser drawer. She was exquisite and at one time had taught Dad ballroom lessons in New York City. Our father had learned of her death while reading the New York paper one Sunday. In shock, he tried to deal with his grief by writing a book about the affair. But once the book was completed, it languished in a closet never to be read, and the mystery has remained unresolved. Meanwhile Dad made some trips to settle issues about her demise. Although the dancer's death was considered a suicide, Dad believed she was murdered.

There was a rumor that our mother found out about Dad's affair when she opened his personal mail—a bad habit she had. Then she read of the impending adoption of his son from an orphanage. Years later, we heard that our half-brother was raised in California. Once the mystery evolved into facts, I often wondered how to find him but had no time or money to search.

On the road again, the old truck sputtered and shook as we climbed through the Rockies, barely making the summit. By the time we reached Salt Lake City, I was about ready to quit the move, settle down, and become a Mormon. On the Salt Lake Desert both the truck and the car got flat tires. Once the tires were repaired, we drove undaunted across Nevada until we crossed the border into California, where I felt a moment of euphoria. Now, as we climbed the Sierras, I briefly lost sight of the truck. Deciding that somehow I had passed my husband, I stopped and waited. We had no backup plans for being lost. Those were the days before smartphones and instant communication. Finally, I drove on and spotted the truck parked by the roadside. Relieved, we again plunged ahead with our next goal: Alcatraz Island, where my father's retired military cousin awaited us. Soon, behind schedule and holding up traffic, we started across the Golden Gate Bridge, and I realized another car was signaling us. The colonel had located us traveling slowly by our out-of-state license plates. He led us to the dock, where we transferred to a boat for Alcatraz. For three days, we enjoyed the company of our host who lived and worked at the prison. After being shown what we were allowed to see of the island, I purchased postcards for friends that read, "Alcatraz Island, wish you were here."

Within a week, my husband secured a job and a rental house. He put a For Sale sign of $400 on the truck, which he promptly sold, and we began our fifteen years of life together in California, which ended with his death. We quickly settled into a two-income, 1960s lifestyle. I had learned that the price of living in this paradise called California required me to work to make ends meet. Eventually we purchased a home of our own and later had two more children. During these years, I learned to love the tempo, the freedom, and the rhythm of California. In New England, people were more private and reserved. Now I felt everyone was a neighbor, accepting and tolerant. I loved the mountains that rose in the distance from our home. I often sat in a rocker and watched the sea fog rise and sit on the top of the peaks like whipped cream. One could not overlook the delightful year-round weather. I thought I would never leave, and indeed I did not until I was married for the fourth time. I also found opportunities to teach ballet at nursery schools and a creative workshop. At last my talents were being utilized.

However, I never could get used to the size of western homes, which, compared to the East, seemed small for our family. I missed the old homes with a basement and an attic. I thought it should all be reversed. We should retire to this one-story, 1,500-square-foot house and enjoy having two bathrooms. When I grew up, we shared one bath at the top of the stairs. Often three of us children would be lined up, sitting impatiently on the stairs waiting our turn. "Mother," we would complain, "Chuck is reading a funny book on the throne."

Our new sixties lifestyle started at six in the morning five days a week when my husband left for a maintenance job. He returned in the late afternoon in time to take over the childcare so I could leave for an assembly job. He would find the evening meal I had prepared for the family on the stove, and when I awoke in the morning, he had reciprocated with breakfast in a double boiler. Our children lived with this arrangement for five years until their father's illness.

Meanwhile our son Bret remained a delightful child with few behavioral problems. However, I was notified again of complaints about his teasing. I thought maybe his slow verbal development could be a cause of his antisocial behavior, and he was referred to a speech therapist. Following six months of evaluation, no conclusive diagnosis was given. "Perhaps," it was suggested, "he has a high-frequency sound loss." In later years, I looked back at these problems, wondering if his early teasing and speech problems were signs of the mental illness that must have frustrated him when he wanted attention.

Bret's behavior reminded me of my mother, who had an uncanny ability to upset me and whose conversations were often provocative and simplistic. She had always aggravated me to the point of tears and often taunted me by saying things such as "You look like a fish when you cry." Like my mother, Bret continued to arouse my ire easily and similarly knew what buttons to push. I remain frustrated by his immature behavior and often upset at my inability to control my emotions when I communicate with him. Even now, years later, when I talk to Bret on the phone, I am aware of my voice rising in pitch during our conversation.

One day Bret came home from grammar school and asked me, "Do you know what s—t means?" "No," I replied. If I did know, I would have reprimanded him. As he matured, he continued the habit of inappropriate conversation to watch my response. He often complained about bodily functions although doctors found nothing wrong with him, and now as a grown man, he continues to worry about physical problems. Unfortunately, like my relationship with my mother, I have never learned to dismiss what I consider offensive or embarrassing in his conversations. It remains a challenge to talk to my son just as it was a problem to control my responses with my mother. Her uncanny ability to upset me remained throughout her life, and the same haunts me now with Bret. Unfortunately, I have never learned how to deal with personalities like theirs, and I have had to accept that inability. Daily I wish for better coping skills in living with difficult people like my mother and son. Now, in later life, I am still groping for control.

Despite his verbal difficulties as a youth, Bret maintained a paper route for several years and handled his own finances. With his money he bought his clothes and personal items. Today, he constantly reminds me of this achievement. One time he bought a used bike from someone on the street. Not long afterward, a police officer knocked on the door and said he was checking on a stolen bike, the one Bret had bought. Nothing more was done when he realized Bret had paid for the bike. The paper route remains one of his few accomplishments in life, along with his later military experience. As a teenager, he also found pride in his ability to ride a motorcycle at a local course where he received several trophies. Long into adulthood, he still asks if I have the trophies.

In elementary school, Bret and his elder sister, Dora, were required to repeat third grade because of speech problems. No definitive diagnosis was ever given for their problems. A wealthy relative paid for Dora to be diagnosed at a hospital in San Francisco. At the time, Dora was receiving speech therapy through the schools, and they were advised of her testing and a possible diagnosis of dyslexia, which was a genetic family disability. Dora was nearly ten years old before I could completely understand her conversation. However, Dora and her father, with whom she had a close relationship, seemed to communicate well. He adored her, and she reciprocated those feelings. For the children, repeating a grade in school was humiliating and a blow to their egos. This, along with their continuing speech problems, left them vulnerable and insecure. Dora, in spite of her unusual beauty, remained self-conscious and somewhat awkward throughout her life. Her insecurity about her appearance was like that of her father, who was uncomfortable with his tall, thin physique.

I encouraged the children to succeed by paying for drum and guitar lessons for Bret and ballet for Dora. All of the children had piano lessons. It was a personal disappointment to me that none of them were musical or artistic, since my love of life had included all the arts: dance, piano, choir, sculpture, voice, and drama. Later I suggested careers to my daughter, but she refused to try anything. Dora always found excuses for being unable to pursue a career. I think she was afraid of failing. As an adult, she did graduate from junior college and completed a bartending class that I paid for.

Meanwhile the two unplanned births of another son and daughter within close proximity made it difficult for my husband and me to maintain a two-income family. Now in my thirties, I was delighted with the expanding family, but my husband, who was ten years older than me, was overwhelmed.

As usual during my pregnancies, I experienced severe morning sickness twenty-four hours a day. In the case of my third child, when I worked as an admitting clerk at a hospital, I was given time off with complete understanding. Following sick leave, I returned to work and stayed until two weeks before my delivery. My doctor reminded me that he was available on staff should I need him.

I was advised to be induced at a hospital, assuring the doctor that I would not go into labor prematurely. It was far more difficult than the earlier home births, and there was none of the privacy and dignity that I enjoyed at home. Following years of separation from my mother, I invited her to visit us for the birth, ensuring that the two younger children had someone with them while I was hospitalized. She was delighted to feel needed and tried hard to be useful during the brief visit. Following the birth, my husband brought my mother to pick me up when I was released. He was so excited when he took me to the car that after seating the baby and me, he forgot the vase of flowers from my mother that he had placed on top of the car. When the car started moving, the vase fell and smashed in the parking lot. Well, I did have the intent to enjoy.

Following the visit with my mother, which went smoothly, she joined my younger brother and his family, who lived a few hours' drive from us. I had planned for her visit with great precautions. Knowing her propensity to rummage through anything personal, I had hidden my personal files in the trunk of my car. During my absence, she had arranged for Bret to become a newspaper boy, which I had never thought of doing. It was a job he held proudly for some years. Finally, I hoped, I had a pleasant experience with my mother.

After she left, I had the opportunity to admire my handsome baby in his crib. I had a premonition, a feeling that he would be special. In childhood, however, he suffered from yearly attacks of pneumonia for which he had to endure frequent penicillin shots. He had extensive testing and was found to be allergic to almost everything listed. One doctor told me that my son would never be strong. I wish that doctor had lived to see the boy grow into a wonderful career marine. Not only did he overcome his weakness but he also survived a number of accidents. The worst incident occurred in childhood at a brother's house. We were visiting for a weekend, and my brother and his wife were out doing errands. Suddenly, there was a crash of glass breaking, and we found my son on the floor with his thigh cut open deeply after putting his knee through a glass patio door. "I'm going to die!" he wailed. He kept crying as someone picked him up and placed him on the kitchen counter where his wound was held together. His poor cousin, who had been chasing him, stood shocked in a corner while I called 911. Soon he was taken to the local hospital where a doctor took a look at him while he finished working on another accident patient. Our son was given a sedative until the doctor could begin cleaning the glass from the large wound before stitching. For the first time, he spent a night in the hospital and was released to travel home the next day.

When he was older, he was riding his bike down our rocky driveway with his dog tied to his handlebars. As he sped down an incline, the dog went one way, and he flew off his bike in another direction onto gravel. I was at the university at the time, so it was his older sister who attended to him and drove him to the emergency room where he again had numerous stitches on his knee.

My fourth baby, another girl, grew up to become a mother and teacher. At birth, she resembled my first daughter: They both had round faces with mops of dark hair that later changed to golden streaks. She and her younger brother have been my pride and joy; both are free of the mental complications of the two older children. My daughter has been independent, sociable, and outgoing. My son has retired from a successful military career and continues working in the field he loves. Both children are married. It has always remained a mystery to me how the two younger children could be so different—and so productive— from the eldest two when they all had the same father.

Sometimes a mother is unfairly blamed for the mental illness of a child, especially a child like my eldest son. But while my first two suffered with severe illness, I have two outstanding younger children. Sometimes I question if it was environment that brought on their illnesses. The first two children were born in the Northeast while the other children were born and raised in California. I also wondered if the loss of the father they loved and remembered so well contributed to the illnesses of the two older children, while the youngest two have little or no memory of him. The youngest child recalls, with some admiration, that the only father she knew well was my third husband.

Following the unexpected birth of a fourth child, the added responsibility of two more children drained our finances. After each birth, I tried to return to work. The United States is not Europe, where many countries give both parents maternity leave to care for a new child. Tragically, not long after the birth of my fourth child, I learned that my husband was terminally ill with a hereditary illness, Lou Gehrig's disease. Under the strain, I no longer felt able to maintain our four-bedroom home, so I downsized and rented a duplex while my husband was placed in a nursing home.

Eventually, the lingering illness of their father compounded the insecurity of the two elder children. Their father languished in the nursing home for nine months, and at his worst stage, he asked me not to bring the children to visit. Bret, however, would ride his bike to see his father. My younger son still has vague memories of seeing his father there in a wheelchair when I took him along to visit.

As my husband was bedridden, I coped with the four children alone, and we talked little about their father's condition. Bret and Dora spent a month with an aunt in Canada one summer when I was stricken with hepatitis. For a while they seemed oblivious to their father's condition. Free from worry, and unaware of their father's declining condition, they relaxed, and at the end of vacation, they were brought back to me by relatives who only complained about their teasing each other.

At this time, I sought psychiatric counseling with little results. My first appointment with a therapist became too personal. Further treatment consisted of joining a large therapy group he led. He continued to pursue me on a personal basis for some time until I sought other outlets for help. I left his final meeting in tears. I learned that a middle-aged widow like me was vulnerable, and I soon became wary of therapists and doctors. I endured several inappropriate encounters until I found other outlets in which to heal and socialize.

Before and after my husband's death, I kept trying to work although the cost of childcare made it entirely impractical. It was while on a new job that I received an unsolicited call from the welfare department. A social worker visited and informed me that my employer was placing me on six months of disability. Following that, I was to be supported by welfare in a college program to obtain my associate of arts degree. Childcare was provided for the two youngest children, who experienced excellent childhood programs. This gave us security and stability. I delighted in the opportunity to attend college since I had always wished for further education, but I had received no encouragement as a child. I chose a program to obtain a teaching credential. However, I was only given a two-year program, which realistically prepared me for little as a single parent. Once, when I was nine years old, I had announced to my mother that I wanted to be a schoolteacher when I grew up. Her reaction was one of total discouragement. She declared, "Only spinsters are teachers." I never brought up the subject again. A childhood girlfriend was encouraged to complete a teaching credential, and when, like me, she was left widowed with children, she was able to be independent. How sad that I was so ill advised and left destitute.

My experiences with welfare were positive. I managed to rent a pleasant three-bedroom apartment for us. Food stamps allowed us to have an adequate diet, and we had medical coverage. Without any help from family or church, we managed to live comfortably. Of course, there were no fast-food meals, and no entertainment, cable, or trips. We never visited a restaurant. We had the basic necessities, which were added to by my monthly trips to the Salvation Army for clothes and attendance at every church potluck. I experimented with vegetarian meals to stretch our diet and spent hours in the local parks to provide entertainment for the two younger children. Bret continued his paper route and purchased what he needed for which he took great pride. This continued until the death of my husband when we left welfare for Social Security benefits. Later, as part of a federal housing plan, I was able to buy a new home.

For years Bret has complained that we moved too much. In retrospect, I regret that we had to be uprooted from familiar neighborhoods so often. I'm also sorry that the children did not have grief support. I now realize that they suffered immensely emotionally. When their father died, the two eldest attended a simple funeral at our church. Only Bret shed tears when I received the early morning call about his father's death. The other children continued sleeping unaware of the tragedy.

Eventually I joined singles groups for companionship, but there was little help for the children. I took them to church, and we continued to frequent the weekly potluck dinners. For one school semester, Bret was sent to live with relatives in a small town in the mountains. They had four children, and I hoped it would be a good change for Bret. In hindsight I regret this because he again had to make difficult adjustments. After one school year, Bret rejoined us.

Within three years of my husband's death, I dated and then married a man I met at church; he had custody of two children and was a good provider. A mutual friend introduced us, and I became aware of the middle-aged man watching me every Sunday when I sang in the church choir. I couldn't help but note that his eyes were on me, scrutinizing my every glance. He had a son the age of Bret and a cute daughter, who hung on to him constantly. Soon my youngest daughter was also hanging on to this new person in our lives. He certainly favored the youngest of my children, who had no memories of a father.

Once we decided to marry, we had a small family wedding and a reception at my house. Because of the proximity of his job to his home, I rented out my house, and we moved into his larger home, where we spent one and a half years. Again my children had to double up: Bret with my husband's son, Dora in her own room, and my youngest daughter sharing a bedroom with my husband's young daughter. My youngest boy had to fit into an improvised, walled-off space in the living room. My children again had to adjust to new schools and a change of environment.

I felt I was not able to be the stepmother I should be, as I had no background experience in taking on such a role, and instead I continued to care for my children as best I could. I felt that my husband and I were trying hard to adjust to a difficult situation. He had a travel trailer that we frequently used to take the children on educational trips. During our marriage, we enjoyed several interesting vacations—with the six children comfortably sleeping together—visiting sites we had never seen before. We climbed mountains and attended lectures by rangers at state parks. It was an experience I could never give my children alone. We also gave the children horseback riding lessons in a park near our home.

During this period, I continued my education by signing up at the local university. With my associate degree behind me, I could look forward to upper-level classes. I not only took these studies but also took one art class at the lower-level junior college that proved to be most interesting. At a local display, we decorated a unique holiday booth of balloons people could jump into, which the family got to see and enjoy.

Once I took a still-life art class and filled my sketchbook with nude drawings. I hid them from my husband, fearing he would not understand my work. Becoming wary of his sudden bursts of rage, I was concerned that he would see my portfolio of nudes and become indignant. For me it was just another requirement filled for my degree. But I continued to hide my work and never talked about the class.

I soon learned that my husband had an unpredictable temper. On one occasion, he beat his son, and when I reached for the phone, he ripped it out of the wall, thwarting my attempt to call 911. On another evening, when he slapped Dora across the face for a simple request concerning a school class, I decided immediately to plan a return to the house I still owned. Despite my physical attraction to my husband, I eventually had to remove my children from his home and was discouraged at ever subjecting them to another stepfather. For a year, my husband and I remained cordial and still did things with the children. It was not until I moved out of the area that I eventually filed for divorce with another marriage on the horizon.

During that second disastrous marriage, Bret failed to graduate with his high school class and my husband's son. When we later moved back to our own home, Bret took the initiative to spend the summer finishing the requirements for the diploma he is still proud of. During high school, he had been trained to work at a gas station, and following graduation he tried to find a similar job to no avail. The jobs had become extinct. With his background, I was surprised when he was accepted into the army where he served driving a truck for three years. Try as he did, this was the last meaningful job he ever had.

3
A New Beginning

With Bret in the army and a failed marriage, I impulsively decided to sell our house and move to the small rural town where I had relatives. I was proud that Bret had cared enough to complete high school and was now in the military. Meanwhile Dora confided that while we lived with my previous husband, she had been sexually involved with a neighbor boy. The encounters occurred while my former husband and I were taking classes together at our church. Dora had been lured into sex with the older boy behind our backs. She remarked that she found the experience distasteful. I was dismayed that I had not been vigilant and realized that great caution must be taken in marriage with a blended family. I doubted that I could ever subject the children to another relationship on my part. It was devastating at times because I had a satisfying relationship with my former husband and did not have to work.

When the house sold, the move north was going as planned until there was unexpected rebellion from Dora, who was not ready to make a change. I realized too late that as their mother, I had never sat and discussed plans and changes in our lives with my children. In retrospect, I attribute this inability to share to the lack of conversation at home during my childhood. Soon after we moved and settled into a rented house, Dora ran away. I watched as she darted through the back woods like a lost fawn and disappeared. I tried to pursue her, but she was gone. When I contacted the local police, they would not help because she had left voluntarily. They would post nothing for a week. Now, under severe duress, I required medical help. I had contended with criticism from Dora's school about her attire. She was asked not to wear a leather jacket to school and to keep her midriff covered. Dora was exotic looking and created a sensation among the local males. I endured scary telephone calls from boys at school and had to keep abreast of others who pursued her. I had few friends and little emotional support living alone in a new town with four children.

Having no idea where she had gone, we waited a week before she returned on her own. I learned that she had gone to our old neighborhood and stayed with a girlfriend until her mother asked Dora to leave. Alone, she had hitched rides both ways—a four-hour trip—and gratefully she survived to tell about it. An older boy helped her leave town by driving her to the highway. I never knew how she became acquainted with that person.

Soon after her return, it became apparent that Dora was not adjusting to the move. It was not until I met my next husband that Dora began to accept the changes. She eventually went to a continuation school where she applied herself assiduously and graduated early from high school. I then gave her our old car so she could attend the local junior college from which she eventually graduated.

Dora's life had been traumatized time and time again. She later wrote that she never wanted to go through the problems I had to experience with marriage and children. In retrospect, I regret the grief she endured, and if I could have changed anything, I certainly would have done so. A mother can't help but feel responsible for protecting her child, and the decisions I made will forever haunt me. Always lingering in my thoughts are the "what ifs." I torment myself, wondering about every decision to move, to marry, and to guide my children.

Soon after Dora returned home, we made a rare visit to Bret at the army base where he was stationed. I was appalled by his distance and the sadness in his expression, and worried about his ability to cope with military life. He appeared to ignore or resent our visit, and I felt he blamed me for a bad decision. He was definitely struggling with his career. He later told me that being in such close contact with people was difficult for him. I concluded that the death of his father combined with military service and separation from home contributed to the onset of his eventual mental illness. While serving as a truck driver in the army, he began to drink for the first time. And he and his friends were demoted for using marijuana. Bret eventually completed his time in the military. Ironically, in later life he regarded his service with the same pride that he held for his paper route.

The job I had accepted when we moved to the small town was terminated, and I filled the void by exploring art lessons at a local shop. One class member befriended me and soon confided that she had terminal cancer and had but a few months to live. She commented that some people avoided her when she mentioned her cancer. She invited the children and me to her lovely mountain home at Thanksgiving, and I met her husband and youngest son. It was months later, following her death, that her husband told me he had decided on my first visit that he would marry me. Since I did sewing on the side, the woman provided me with some work and later brought her husband along to pick up the finished items. As predicted, she died after Christmas, and her husband contacted me to sing at her funeral. After thirty-five years of marriage, he was devastated and visited me regularly for solace. One day he sat and cried, which may have released much of his stress after months of caregiving. He often picked me up where I worked and took me to a restaurant or prepared a lunch at his house. Within months, our relationship became serious, and he asked us all to move into his large home, where he was lonely. During my first months in his home, I received a call from one of his relatives who expressed objections to our relationship. She said, "It is too soon."

Months after our move into his home, he asked me to go to Reno for a quick marriage. I learned that grown children often object to the love life and decisions of their parents, so we married with no fanfare. This problem became evident years later when I again married a widower with grown children. On both occasions, my marriages were entirely private. I have always yearned to be dressed in a white bridal gown and think that someday I may rent a dress and pose for a picture.

Once we settled into my husband's large home, he began making renovations to create spaces for my three children. Downstairs he partitioned a long room with a wall that gave my youngest son his own room for the first time. It was planned that Dora and her sister would share a large bedroom also on the lower level. At last, my family and I felt some stability in our lives. As a government retiree, my husband provided us with security, and we were able to live in one place while the three remaining children completed school and college. Not until my children were grown and my husband was terminally ill did we downsize at the end of a twenty-year marriage. His two eldest children have remained close friends in my life.

By this time, his two eldest and my Dora seemed content. She applied herself to completing high school a year early to compensate for the grade she had earlier repeated. Then she went on to the local junior college and graduated but with no goals in mind. After leaving home, she spent two more years at a college while working a small job, serving coffee at a restaurant. When Dora turned eighteen, she started receiving her portion of the Social Security death benefits from her father. I had depended on this allotment to raise the children and had expected the money to last until each child reached the age of twenty-two. However, this benefit was gradually cut back each year by the government and soon ended. Dora, however, received her expected money long enough to spend four years in college. My younger children saw the amounts cut and finally done away with by age eighteen, which left the two youngest children struggling to attend school beyond junior college.

Prior to our marriage, my husband had decided that he would not take on a father role with my children. He explained that he had raised four children and seen them all graduate from college. His two girls were married, a son was in the navy, and his youngest son headed to law school. Retired, he preferred not to intervene in my affairs but his presence was all the guidance we needed. He was known to be a strict, controlling, and private person who never lost his temper. A conservative man, he involved himself in local government. My youngest daughter grew up respecting his calm control and intelligence. However, Dora had some early adjustments to his authority. One day, she loudly confronted my husband in front of his son. "You are not my father," she said. I was busy in the kitchen and didn't understand what had precipitated the outburst. All I could surmise was that she wanted to assert where she stood in the family arrangement in front of his son. My husband's children would never speak that way to their father, whom they respected but felt was too controlling. Dora made her point, and my husband just looked shocked.

Only once during my marriage did any of the children mention their late father. My husband became briefly involved with the Boy Scouts for my younger son. One summer, he went to camp with him, but something occurred there that upset him, and he returned to his earlier hands-off status with my son. One day, following a problem, I found my son sitting on the ground on a bluff crying, "I want my dad." He missed the father he barely knew but realized my husband would never be the father he longed for.

I recall these years when Dora lived with us as a tranquil time for her. She had her weight variations, which I never understood. She ate like a horse at home, and when we went to a restaurant, she ordered the most expensive items on the menu. It was only when she was grown that she confided to me that she had bulimia during her adolescence.

Soon after marrying, my husband encouraged me to finish my college degree at the local university. I was delighted and continued studies for several years. Later, on two occasions, Dora and I took classes together. I was short on science credits, so I enrolled in classes with her. While I came home from classes and started preparing for dinner, Dora was applying herself to studying extra hard. I was delighted when she got better grades than I did in both classes. She beamed and became more self-assured. I hoped my eventual graduation with a master's degree was an example for my children. Three of them attended my graduation from the university. Eventually they completed high school and graduated from the local junior college. Also, my youngest son became active in the local Masonic Temple and had many friends. I felt criticism from others that my husband never attended any of the Masonic events at which my son officiated. I was called upon to arrange dinners and ceremonies without his help.

Although the children grew up without a father, they continued to adapt well. The day after my youngest son graduated from high school, he joined the marines and left for boot camp. My youngest daughter and I attended his graduation and then went to Disneyland before driving him to his next assignment. He spent the next two years in college while serving in the reserves. After that he went into full-time duty and retired after twenty-five years of service.

Following her youngest brother's example, my younger daughter also graduated from junior college. She then took a class in travel for which her stepfather loaned her the money, and she found work from a friend who owned an agency. However, restless from living in a small town, she followed her military brother to Hawaii where he was stationed several times between duties in Iraq. She obtained a waitress job in the officers' mess on the marine base. One day, she waited on a marine who felt she looked overwhelmed with her new life in Hawaii. They soon became friends and eventually married. Her husband also served as a career marine. Their service gave them great opportunities to see the world and to learn skills. Following the births of two children, my daughter returned to college and graduated with a teaching credential.

One of the fears I had while raising my children was that I might become like my mother, who was described as "difficult." I thought I would rather die than submit my children to a similar ordeal. As a teenager, I was driven close to suicide more than once. I remember my mother pacing the floor and saying, "Leave me alone. I am going out of my mind." She had been a social butterfly, always nervous about the responsibilities she assumed as chairman or president of numerous organizations. Mother seemed to have two personalities: one was social and friendly in public, and the other was nervous and unpleasant with us when our father was not home.

I also worried that my university studies were depriving the children of my attention. However, my graduation from college did set an example for them, and three eventually graduated from college.

By this time in my life, my doctor had put me on Prozac and then Paxil, which I have intermittently used most of my life. Along with these I became addicted to clonazepam to sleep and have used it for over forty years. A nervous condition, hyperventilation, which started when I moved west, continued to frustrate me. Episodes occurred whenever I tried to entertain or speak in public. This, along with frequent hiccups I'd had from infancy, worried me. At various times I sang professionally, and fears of these nervous conditions haunted me. It was with immense determination that I completed a master of arts degree in college and then started teaching and speaking publicly. At the same time, I was struggling to cope with constant emergencies involving Bret. My husband could tell when I skipped my meds because I became impatient and easily upset. He would gently ask, "Have you taken your pills?"

With a degree and a new marriage, I began to emerge from my shell. My first experiences in college enabled me to blossom, to become the person I had dreamed of being. For the first time, I was able to express my opinions and be heard. In occupational tests, I scored highest as an author and artist. After studying quilting in art classes and joining a local guild, I was asked to teach and was recognized for teaching quilt classes. I taught at college and recreation departments, and in stores. I also had several quilt books published, I appeared in shows, and I sold my own patterns. One contest included appearing at Dollywood for an annual quilt show, which led to making some pillows for Dolly Parton one Christmas.

However, I still required psychiatric help, and one doctor told me, "Your family has emotionally assassinated you." Today I doubt that she would say that, for with college graduation I felt I had come out of my cocoon, spread my wings, and evolved into a vivacious, talkative person—like a butterfly that has emerged from a dark cavern.

I was confident that I did not exhibit most of the mental conditions my mother had. She was the most nervous person I have ever met and was later diagnosed with panic disorder. Her sister had stated that Mother was "crazy." My aunt often told me stories of their childhood, such as when my mother hid during a storm and my aunt, nine years younger, would comfort her.

I also realized that when my mother made a rare visit, anything personal still had to be hidden. When she stayed with us, I locked our financial files in the trunk of my car to avoid her going through them while I was absent. Following visits with my brothers, she would comment on many of their personal affairs. It was also obvious that when she visited my aunt, she would go through her closet because she described in detail her large collection of stiletto shoes. Once, when she was a guest in our home, my husband intercepted her attempts to look at income-tax papers he had sprawled over the dining table. He foiled her curiosity at seeking information on our personal matters.

Mother also had the habit of sneaking about to listen to conversations. At a family reunion, my sister found her hidden close by, trying to hear our chatter. When I was at home, she would listen to my phone conversations and often mimic me. Relatives found it disconcerting that she often stood outside of the bathroom when they occupied it. I'm not sure of a diagnosis for her personality other than nosy, impolite, and insecure, or maybe she just had an unhealthy mind. No matter what, she constantly embarrassed us. Of the seventeen grandchildren my parents had, Mother took interest in one whom she adopted and accepted into her home for a period.

A funny thing happened when one of my brothers and his wife were visiting Mother. My sister-in-law had carefully laid out her false eyelashes in order on the bedspread while she took a shower. Predictably, Mother slipped into the room to look around, and thinking the eyelashes were dust, she brushed them all onto the floor. She had one upset daughter-in-law to confront afterward. The irony is that Mother was never apologetic but rather smirked as if it was a joke. She seemed to take pleasure in upsetting everyone.

None of my children had phobias like my mother had, but I learned too late that Dora was depressed and perhaps bipolar. Her doctors had missed any abnormalities she might have exhibited. Since her early teens, Dora had spent hours on her appearance before going to school. She would get up as early as four o'clock to start the long ritual of doing her makeup. I noticed that she plucked her thick eyebrows into a hard, narrow shape. Then each of her eyelashes were carefully covered with mascara and separated with a pin. For years, she wore her long auburn hair parted in the middle and straight around her shoulders, resembling the famous Mona Lisa. When we wanted to go out as a family, we always had to wait for Dora. Her clothing was very sixties and intentionally showed off her slender, five-foot-four figure. Her usual choice of jeans fit her slender legs like tights. When we went shopping, I was aware of the stares she received from others customers, and I sensed that Dora was self-conscious about the illusion she had worked so laboriously to create.

At various times, I sought professional help with raising Dora. One therapist asked me how I would describe my daughter. I thought and was blank. All I could say was "She is beautiful." This was not an adequate answer, but I could think of nothing else. Dora's personality was described as "flat." She expressed no emotion, was distant, and had few friends. She reminded me of an aunt who was religious, unemotional, and rigid. I thought Dora definitely took after her father's side. In later life, we learned that the aunt suffered from depression. She was simple and had little education, but she was kind and dependable. Her life ambition was to be able to "speak in tongues." Dora had no such ambitions, but like her aunt she had dark moments.

In contrast to Dora, my youngest daughter maintained a respectable sporty style that suited her personality. She is outgoing, sociable, and popular. Unfortunately, she could have spent more time on schoolwork if it were not for her social life. When she had a serious relationship with a Mormon boyfriend, she became baptized in his church. Later, when she married a Catholic, she converted to his faith. But to this day, regardless of her beliefs, she remains a delightful, charming person who has made me proud. While in school she had two attacks of mononucleosis that required hospitalization and set her back a year in school. Like Dora, she graduated on time by attending a special school that allowed her to catch up.

My children enjoyed horseback riding, and for a year, I rented a horse that the girls had to care for at a stable. Sometimes they went together to a local riding stable and rode a horse to our house. My younger daughter participated in a riding club and shows for some years. She also had a large collection of toy horses. Every Christmas, my husband took the three children into the woods to pick out a Christmas tree. They loved decorating it. I never heard my children complain about this marriage throughout the twenty years we had together. We had a beautiful home in the mountains where we experienced serenity and peace.

By now my children each had their own room since the youngest moved upstairs to a small guest room. The girls found some of my husband's restrictions difficult: for instance, they both liked to wash their hair in the shower each night, and my husband was fanatic about saving our well water. He heated water with a solar panel and the house with a potbellied stove. Like most teenagers, washing hair was a ritual. After the girls complained about the lack of water pressure, I discovered that he had turned it to low. He never realized that I opened it up for more power. In his further attempts to be thrifty, he insisted on clothes being dried on a line instead of using the dryer. I had to continually balance the positive against the negative. There were many inconveniences to overlook to make the family congenial. I never did solve the problem of the dryer. His son complained about the stiff towels, and I had to explain that I could not make them soft without using the dryer. But these were small inconveniences considering his generosity. My doctor once surprised me by commenting, "I have heard that your marriage is not all that great." I responded, "Doctor, I have put thirteen years into this marriage, and I intend to remain in it." I don't think he understood my options. Here I was blessed with compatibility and mutual respect versus welfare. Fortunately, I saw my husband through his final illness and death. He left me financially independent as a reward.

My younger son remained focused at school and with his DeMolay activities. He had become a fine public speaker and was traveling locally for the organization as a master counselor. My husband and I trusted the children enough to take an occasional trip, including one to Hawaii and several to his home in Wisconsin. At such times, I would hire an older girl to stay with the family. My stepsons sometimes visited us on weekends and made themselves at home. I was pleased that the youngest son always headed to my cookie jar to partake of my homemade treats. He and his older brother spent Thanksgiving, and Christmas with us. Once they were married, I enjoyed seeing some of their youngsters grow up from birth. After my earlier disastrous marriage, I found that we could have a happy life in a blended family.

4

Falling Through the Cracks

The ordeal of caring for Bret increased when he left the military following three years of service. Until that time, my new husband had never met my elder son. Coincidentally, his younger son had been born the same week as Bret. But, unlike Bret, he had goals and was in college, studying to become an attorney.

Although my husband had kindly accepted my three younger children, he was not prepared to help Bret, who was an adult. My husband's home was large, but we had already walled off sections of the downstairs to make room for three children. While dating my husband, he had asked me, "What can I use the downstairs for, especially the long fifty-foot room?" Kidding, I suggested a bowling alley. At that time, my husband's youngest son was still living at home following the death of his mother. When my husband moved us into the house, his son soon moved out close to campus in the next town.

Soon I had the unexpected return of Bret to contend with after he completed his military duty. I had always expected him to move on with a job, work, or a career. His inability to function independently soon became inexplicable to me. No one knew how to help him, and I had no one to turn to. When he finished his military service, he drove to join us, and not far from the house, his car broke down. He walked the remaining distance along a canyon to our house. He arrived disgruntled and barely comprehensible. He acted as though life had wronged him, and he never thought about possible causes for his dilemma. Once the car was towed to a garage, it was discovered that Bret had left a jacket on the engine, and it had become entangled with the motor in such a way that it could not be salvaged. He then moved in with us, an adult with no car and no job. The next few months were filled with his failed attempts to find work. Bret had no plans or ideas of what to do in the future. Meanwhile my husband's son, who was in college, continued to visit us on weekends with piles of books that he studied constantly. He eventually obtained his law degree and moved to Washington DC.

Then my husband's eldest son returned after completing six years in the navy. He spent some time with us before seeking work in the more lucrative job market of a larger city, as there was little hope of finding a meaningful job in the retirement area where we lived.

Frustrated, my husband soon insisted that Bret live elsewhere, so I moved him to a hotel in the next town hoping he would find himself. This move began a seven-year nightmare for me while Bret drifted and was unable to maintain a job. He tried local programs providing manual work but was unable to cope. He moved away to join his elder sister, only to lose jobs and drift Sometimes he returned to the university town near us and tried working at a gas station only to be fired. Others his age were active in their pursuit of an education or skills, but Bret was drifting aimlessly and hopelessly. Meanwhile his sister Dora was in the metropolis and seemed able to survive on her own.

During this period, I continued to support Bret with money for food and lodging. It was after he had two accidents on a bicycle that I was made aware of his problem with alcoholism. One night I was notified that he was in the hospital; he had driven his bike into a parked car and was injured. On another occasion, I was informed that he was in the hospital following an accident on his bike when he tangled with a road sign and was injured. It was during this admittance to the hospital that a doctor diagnosed him with a drinking problem. His roommate, a caring pastor, relayed the diagnosis to me, and I finally realized that Bret was ill. Following the accident, I went to the apartment where Bret had been residing and cleaned up his room and his bath, which was covered with vomit from alcohol sickness. Later, while Bret was working briefly at a social agency for the disabled, it was again confirmed that he was abusing alcohol.

Having never confronted alcohol abuse before, I was at a loss how to help. I had heard rumors that my paternal grandfather, whom I never met, had been a "gentleman drinker." I reached out to agencies, such as Alcoholics Anonymous, for help. Bret tried attending their meetings but discovered that he was unable to join in the conversation. AA meetings encouraged participants to speak in a group, which was terrifying to Bret. He actually had to drink alcohol to gain the courage to attend meetings.

I tried attending AA meetings for families but found it depressing. Many of the attendees were involved in abusive relationships at home, which was difficult to relate to for those of us who experienced few similar experiences. I had contended with verbal and emotional abuse but not physical. Bret and I continued to seek supportive groups for several years. By this time, it was apparent that he was disabled and dependent on me.

Bret began to constantly lose his bikes until I realized that he was selling his belongings for alcohol, his medication of choice. Not only did his bikes disappear, but it also was evident that he was losing his clothes, shoes, and anything he could pawn. He found his way to the local university pub, where he never fit in but could easily sell things. I learned early in dealing with him that I could not give him money. To this day, I only buy gift certificates for him, hoping that my money goes for food or clothes. Bret started a lifetime habit of asking me for a dollar or possibly taking it without my knowledge. I found it difficult to buy him gifts since he could turn things into cash. Bret continues to obtain money when needed. They call it panhandling. I remember this when people approach me on the street since they too might be using money for alcohol or drugs. I prefer to help those in need with tangible items, such as used clothes and furnishings.

Bret also started visiting bars until kicked out. Once, in the next town, I found him severely beaten and abandoned by college students in a rented house. Luckily I had stopped to check on him and discovered him passed out, lying on a mattress on the floor covered with vomit. In the other room, a gas heater had been left on and was leaking fumes. I got Bret into my car and drove him to the emergency room, where I broke down in tears. For years, problems like these continued to plague me as I attempted to help him. Often his problems conflicted with my plans; just as I was expected at an important engagement or was working, he would show up and compromise my job. Once, when I found him with a black eye, I had the police document the incident with photos. After yet another bike accident, Bret was hospitalized with leg injuries and dismissed on crutches. With a cast on his leg and no one to care for him, my husband relented and allowed him to stay at our home. He could obtain no alcohol and was his own amusing self.

During the seven-year period that Bret drifted and fell through the cracks, I insisted on providing him with food and lodging. I even purchased an old station wagon for him to sleep in and parked it adjacent to the police station. I briefly rented a store, also next to the police office, where I conducted some business and let him sleep there at night. During this period, an acquaintance who had lost a son took pity on us and allowed Bret to sleep in a cabin at his car lot.

Finally, my husband suggested that Bret be tested by a professional. Bret complied but found it difficult to concentrate on the written test. Once the tests were completed, the results startled me. The diagnostic evaluation determined that Bret had paranoid schizophrenia with moderate mental retardation. Why had it taken seven years to see the obvious? I was shocked and numb. The wonderful, perfect child who had brought us so much joy when young was now sick. Friday the thirteenth seemed real. I had never considered caring for an ill child. This was not the norm.

I had an uncle who had been diagnosed with the same illness after he was forced into early retirement. I knew him only as a relative who was handsome, dignified, and married with several children. He had spent years in mental hospitals and endured twenty-four electric shocks. He was released in the sixties with the discovery of new medications to which he responded well. Bret, however, did not fit my uncle's criteria, and the state hospitals had all been closed during the sixties.

With an illness confirmed, my husband became more sympathetic but still did not allow Bret to live with us. All future decisions were now up to me. I was warned that Bret would never marry or work in his life. I was directed to obtain lifetime disability benefits for him. I felt alone, as I had throughout my life, without anyone to turn to. As always, I faced the challenges before me with persistence. Because of my life experiences, I never shared or sought help from others. Instead I became wary of people, whether it was family or friends, because too often I had been mistreated, misunderstood, and let down. Even my parents were not aware of my problems. As my father once commented after I shared something with him, "Why can't we have some good news?" I felt that people only wanted to hear positive things. Besides, it appeared to me that everyone had his or her own problems and demons to contend with. Also my family life had been filled with lies, misinterpretations, and misrepresentations.

So I delved into the arduous task of getting my son public assistance. The system required a diagnosis from three doctors, interviews, and endless paperwork. I felt much as I did when applying for my master's degree. Anyone ill could not work through the maze of requirements and appointments necessary to obtain disability help. It requires a strong advocate to complete the mounting demands of applying for assistance. I sensed condemnation as the mother of a mentally ill son. Months were spent in visits to the local mental health agency, where I felt that I was also being evaluated. I certainly did have a lot of baggage. The days turned into months, and I kept wading through a deluge of tasks for my sick son. After six months, Bret started receiving his meager but welcome Social Security checks.

With this income, I decided to buy property where I could house my ill son. This became another albatross around my neck, for I now had a house and acreage to care for. During the next eighteen years, this became both a help and a hindrance for me. The old house I purchased from a friend was on a main street in town and close to stores, without any adjacent neighbors. Bret could shop for himself and get around town on his own. My three younger children also utilized the large place for convenience when attending college. For the next two decades, the house remained a home for Bret and a last resort for the other children when in need. For me it was an added expense that required me to work at various local, low-paying jobs.

However, the yard at the house, one and a third acres of tangled weeds and brush, became a place where I could disappear and work out my frustrations. During the rainy season, the grounds often flooded from an adjacent brook through the property, but I soon found solace in gardening and clearing the years of growth on the land. Unfortunately, none of the children took an interest in the work. Even when I tripped and fell into the brook, I got up and kept digging and clearing, taking pride in every patch of weeds I removed. Yard work became my therapy, and I purchased a weed trimmer and other equipment to attack my project.

Eventually Dora found refuge in the house, but her only contribution to the place was her rescue of rabbits, which her new boyfriend fed to his large snake. The house had an old shed and an abandoned trailer behind it. Both of these became hiding places for some of Bret's homeless friends. In the shed, I once found a suitcase filled with cross-dressing clothes. My solution to the problem was to have a six-foot fence placed on part of the property to discourage drifters from using the building which I eventually got rid of. For years, my son continued to attract friends to his special place, his oasis beside a mulberry tree on the side of the house. Sitting within view of the street, he and his buddies became familiar to the police who would stop when they saw trouble.

Despite my son's diagnosis, he continued to fall through the cracks, and I felt abandoned by society. As his mother, I faced alienation and condemnation and prayed not to become bitter. I wondered if I could ever have a life of my own. My husband was now facing medical problems, first a triple bypass and later cancer. My relatives, I realized, were immersed in their own problems so I rarely contacted them. Occasionally, I hired a brother whom I trusted and felt comfortable with to do carpentry and yard work.

When my father visited prior to his death from cancer, he questioned why Bret, a tall, husky fellow, could not work. With all of his education, he hadn't the vaguest idea what mental illness was about. It was futile to hope friends or family could understand what Bret's condition entailed and what I endured. As I had learned in childhood by living with the sickness and abuse of my mother, there was no one to talk to. The burden was mine alone.

In our small retirement community, it was embarrassing to have the local newspaper publish every police encounter with the public in the daily news. Bret's name was listed frequently, whether for riding a bike drunk or for public intoxication. Embarrassed, I kept these problems from my parents who lived far removed from us. Unfortunately, they heard of the problems from a relative who referred to Bret as "the town drunk."

My life was always on hold; I could be called day or night to pick up Bret at a hospital, the police station, or the local jail. He had constant court appearances that took up most of the day, and I was forced to get him to and from appointments. Prior to court dates, he had to see a public defender. Most professionals were sympathetic but unable to suggest solutions to the problems. Court appearances became a regular ritual. We had to appear at about eight o'clock in the morning. Then we proceeded to the calendar posted in the lobby, which provided us with schedules, names, and times to be heard. Once court opened the doors, the chamber quickly filled with the accused, their families, and staff. Often the defenders were left to make quick final directions to their clients. Sometimes they had never met the accused until they showed up in court. There reached a time when Bret had appeared so often before the same judge that she called me into her chambers for consultation. She recommended that Bret be sent to an agency or a hospital. Upon calling both, I discovered that each one had no room and each referred me to the other. A doctor in one city commented, "No judge can tell me who to admit to my hospital." I met only dead ends even with a judge's court order.

The first time Bret was handcuffed in court and taken to jail, I went to my car and collapsed. I drove to the local mental health facility where I was taken into a room with a therapist. I felt Bret did not belong in jail, but I had no options. Instead of compassionate treatment we were both being punished. The county had a separate jail for alcoholics, which was clean and open. The inmates had bunk beds in a large room, a library, and a cafeteria where family could visit. I'm sure that for many this was a better alternative than the streets. My problem with the jail was that alcoholics were usually picked up during the day, allowed to sober up, and then put out on the street at two o'clock in the morning. The jail was located outside of town, and no transportation existed at that hour. I lost track of the times I was awakened at two o'clock and expected to drive the country roads to the jail to pick up Bret. There was no alternative then. Being abandoned in the country at night could be dangerous. Years later, when we moved to a large city, Bret was given a transportation voucher to get home after being in jail.

For eighteen long years following his diagnosis, I was on emergency call for constant problems at the old house. Sometimes the police responded to public nuisance complaints there. I recall one time when I found Bret so drunk, he was doing a jig in the center of the road. Another time he entered the main house, where his younger sister was living, and broke a door and a chair. She called me, frightened and distressed. Eventually my husband renovated the old house so Bret had a separate apartment away from the main house, which my other children sometimes used. Although he could not bother others now, Bret still annoyed them by banging on walls or going behind the house and screaming. When I first heard the yells, I thought a woman was being attacked in our woods. I soon learned that he had this strange habit of howling like a hurt animal late at night, even when he later lived in the city.

Bret once found a girlfriend through AA, who eventually moved in with him. Her father, a retired colonel, paid her expenses. His only son had been killed in Vietnam, and his wife was dying of cancer. Although he flew into town to visit his daughter, I never met him. His daughter's sojourn at the house was difficult for me. My husband and I recorded the messes the two left about the house. Filth and junk were everywhere. Bret liked to cook but never clean up, and I found leftover, rotten food in the refrigerator and on the counters. In desperation I sometimes went into his apartment when he was absent and cleaned up the mess. It was during these times that I would discover my garden tools stored under his bed. I kept missing my shovels and rakes, along with hammers, and I found Bret had hidden them all for protection. He had become so paranoid that he kept these items for protection along with his dog.

My only reprieve from worry about Bret was when he was sent to jail and the one time he was released on six month's electronic surveillance. Then, while he could not obtain alcohol, I was responsible for purchasing his food. When Bret was placed in a veterans hospital for a month of treatment, he took one day after release to be drunk. All care seemed to become a revolving door with no end in sight. *How*, I wondered, *was my grandfather cared for when he drank?* No one would ever discuss the skeletons in my closet.

Writing about these events years later, I ask myself if I could have dealt with the situation differently. Today, as then, I feel abandoned and alone. But I remember my father saying, "There is always someone worse off." As every day brought more drama and fear, however, I withdrew as I did when a child, choosing to seek comfort in privacy. Those around me had their own demons to fight. Complaining to others seemed like an imposition and a burden no one wanted. Therefore, I withdrew into my hobbies and art projects when I could. During this period, I had a burst of artistic accomplishment, including the publication of quilt books, patterns, and art pieces. My problem was that I was not available to travel and promote my works as most artists did. Along with caring for Bret, I had an ailing husband and obligations I could not deny. Life, I realized, is not fair, and we take the good with the bad. Unfortunately, I had become traumatized and would bear the scars forever.

5

Out of the Woodwork

The years I spent taking care of Bret in the old house were an experience I would never wish on anyone. Along with my son's constant problems, I had to contend with friends he attracted like a magnet to drink with him under the mulberry tree. Each carried his or her baggage of hopelessness, failure, and tragedy.

Bret entertained his friends sitting on lawn chairs on the side of the house near his room, where they talked and drank beer while piling the cans on a windowsill. They would pass hours in the little oasis facing the street, listening to music and commiserating about whatever these unemployed people could talk about. The parade of mostly men who found this corner was constant. They varied widely in ages. When I bought the house, I did not anticipate that so many lost souls would flow in and out of our lives there. There was the occasional parolee, but most were alcoholics, some were drug addicts, and others were hopelessly ill and lonely.

One fellow, who frequented the house for several years, was bipolar. He was intelligent, gifted, and poetic. George had lost his parents in a car crash, had attended college where he excelled, had served in the military, and was now an alcoholic. Over several years, he appeared and disappeared in rapid succession. Eventually we learned that he sometimes checked himself into a veterans hospital for treatment, which gave him a respite from living on the street since he could not maintain a rental.

When George was released from the hospital, he often would show up at Bret's place and ask to hang out until his next disability check arrived. One time he fell and lay on the driveway drunk. A passerby reported this to the police, who checked on him. Another time he began to develop heart problems and collapsed on our couch. An ambulance rushed him to the hospital, and the last news we heard of him was that he had passed away. George, like many of my son's friends, died prematurely for lack of care. I wished that I could have provided a tent for George, but I faced a daily challenge with my own son. It was then that I realized I could have taken in dozens of lost people attracted to the old house, each one living with their own skeletons from their past.

Another young man who found sanctuary sitting under the mulberry tree appeared like others, out of the woodwork. He had a lovely twin sister who stopped occasionally to admonish him to seek help. For a while he managed to hold down a job somewhere doing repairs. Since the house was now empty except for Bret, he asked to rent a room. This quickly became a disaster. Before I realized it, he had piled discarded junk in our yard, behind the house, and in his room. He also brought an abandoned trailer filled with wood to the house and parked it there. Because he had paid rent, I was forced to go to court to evict him. He caused problems for weeks as I worked through the legal system to remove him. Meanwhile, he taunted me while sitting for hours in a lounge chair in the side yard after stopping his rent payments. In desperation, I removed the door to the apartment so he had no privacy, and he soon left.

Once the renter was gone, I had the expense of removing the trailer and all of the junk he had accumulated. It took weeks to pile stuff into my station wagon and haul it to the dump. I found that he was living in the woods behind the house until he suddenly disappeared from our lives. The rooms Bret occupied continued to become filthy from his habit of leaving rotten food and dirty dishes around. I found everything covered with mold and spoiled food in his refrigerator. Most of his pots and pans were left unwashed. His dog also added to the smell. When the police were called to the house, they covered their faces and nearly gagged on the stench. Again in desperation, I pulled up the carpet and put down a tile floor that could be wiped. The police continued to stop at the house to follow up on complaints or break up fights that erupted. Sometimes they called an ambulance and took Bret to a hospital to be treated. However, he always returned, and we started our lives over and over again. Meanwhile he continued to hide my tools under his bed, drink under the mulberry tree, and howl in the woods.

For several years, Dora lived at the house as she tried to get her life in order. When she later moved into her own apartment, I became aware of unscrupulous characters showing up to take what they could from Bret. He still had a motorcycle, which amazingly he had been able to balance on despite his illness unlike two of my nephews who were killed on motorcycles. I wondered if Bret had developed an uncanny sense of survival from the struggles of life he encountered without his father. While in the army, he had driven trucks and never had an accident with his bike, but with his drinking and illness, he was vulnerable. He seemed to be unaware of the dangers some friends were to him, and he could not discern when he was being used. One night, a neighbor, a parolee, brought some men over to visit at the house. From what I could understand, he took Bret out and got him drunk. Meanwhile the other characters stole his motorcycle. Days later, it turned up in the next town abandoned. It was never in a condition to ride again.

Later, after Dora died, I realized Bret could not live alone in the house. Since he was not allowed to live with me in the townhouse I owned, I had no alternative but to sell the place I loved and move into the old house beside Bret. This led to four years of proximity to my mentally ill son with daily concerns and constant care. His friends still sat under the mulberry tree, but there were limits on what they could do to Bret with me around.

During my time in the old house, I continued to enjoy the place and the yard. I had room to carry on with my hobby of quilt design. Following my husband's death, I had joined a hospice where I made friends and had some social life. The few times I resorted to taking Bret to the ER were when meat bees stung him. They were all around, and he had a severe reaction to them. Much of my time now was spent renovating the old place so I could be free from Bret and his noises.

One weekend, his dog got loose and ran into the street where it was hit. Again I was left to pick up the expenses. Bret was fond of his dog and needed him, so I allowed the dog to be cared for. He returned with one leg in a sling for the next few weeks. Later, when Bret was removed from the house, the dog went with him only to be lost. With my presence at the old house, fewer characters appeared to share the space with Bret. The cans still piled up on the windowsill, but there were fewer calls to the police. By this time, I realized that taking Bret to the ER for drinking always resulted in him being sent to jail in the next town. This required me to make the trip at night to pick him up. I was therefore left with the alternative of letting him bang and howl in his apartment while I tried to bury myself in another area of the house.

I had bought the old house as the only option I had for finding shelter for Bret. There were no care homes for the mentally ill. Hospitals for the mentally ill had been closed with the assumption that the states would pick up the slack. This never occurred, and families like me had to face the problems alone.

Earlier I had joined AMI, the local Alliance of the Mentally Ill, and we grew to about forty members. Our meetings consisted of potlucks and speakers. As years passed with no obvious changes in the situations our sick family members endured, our numbers dwindled. I think we became discouraged. I grew tired of the speakers who repeated what we already knew, and the obvious fact that nothing was done or ever would be done. In time we disbanded, left alone with our individual problems. By then I had a younger son in Iraq and other problems to face.

As some characters continued to come out of the woodwork to sit with Bret under the tree, I faced an unknown future caring for my sick, drunk son. My younger son's best friend had been killed on his motorcycle while my son was at sea with the marines. Years passed, and Bret managed to survive against all odds. He drank as though life would go on forever, and I wondered how many more tragedies I would encounter while I lived in the old house with my birds, dog, cats, and ill son. The walls became quieter, and I learned to live alone with the tragedies. Dora was gone; she had tried her wings in the city and was proud of her apartment and jobs. However, we all missed something when we let her take off on her own to search for a future with her boyfriend, Rob. None of us had seen the signals from Rob, which meant that he was moving on without Dora. Had I understood, I would not have helped her leave. Instead I occupied the old house and tried to make it a home without my daughter and to live one day at a time with Bret and his alcoholism. Even the mulberry tree dropped berries for me to pick up along with the beer cans and trash from odd visitors. When I looked at the tall trees and felt the breeze in the yard, I sometimes thought I could be happy there forever. Dora's rabbits were now gone, but I had my own pets to enjoy while I tried to forget that Bret was close by and perhaps sleeping off a hangover. If only fewer characters would come out of the woodwork, maybe I could survive.

6

Dora's Struggles

Following her graduation from junior college, Dora decided to leave our small town and move to the city where she had lived as a child. Her first attempts at job hunting there were not productive although she did make a contact for sharing an apartment. Shortly after she returned home, a girl called and offered Dora the room. Soon she was packed and leaving for what became a ten-year odyssey of life on her own as a single woman in the big city.

After moving in, however, Dora discovered that her new roommate, a law student, was involved with one of her professors and was pregnant. The circumstances being awkward for Dora, she soon moved into the apartment of a drummer friend, which began a tumultuous five-year relationship. With the help of his mother and Dora's part-time waitressing, they managed to maintain a nice apartment. Most of the furnishings were discards from my old house, which made it cozy and complete.

During this period in the city, Dora had her portrait taken, which depicted a now mature, sophisticated young woman. She proudly gave me a large framed rendition that I hung in our guest bedroom. One day, as I stood staring at the portrait, I saw something in her expression that I had not detected previously. I saw sorrow in her vacant stare. Her attempt at a faint smile reminded me of the Mona Lisa. Transfixed, I repeatedly returned to gaze at the portrait. Something about the eyes was not right. For the first time, the word *depression* haunted me. I had no clue about what I should or could do. It only confirmed what I later saw as part of the puzzle of Dora.

Once, when she was visiting, I had her join her sister, who was having class pictures taken. I wanted another photograph of Dora, but this never worked out. The photographer complained to me that something seemed wrong with Dora's eyes when he tried to take a photograph. Eventually I learned that her odd gaze was typical of a drug user. Following this episode, I only received pictures of my happy, wholesome, younger daughter from the local photographer.

While in the city, Dora continued to take college classes until her Social Security benefits ran out. From then on, she experienced a roller coaster of problems with various jobs and her lifestyle. She was described as a "party girl" and once complained to me that her years of attending nightclubs with their loud music had impaired her hearing. During her ten-year sojourn in the metropolis, she managed to remain independent financially with various jobs. However, near the end of her stay with her drummer friend, he began to call me about her deteriorating mental condition. Once, early on an Easter Sunday, after a distress call, I made the four-hour drive to the city to find her still in bed and inconsolable. At the end of a futile day, I had to return to the mountains with nothing accomplished. On one of my future overnight visits, while Dora's boyfriend was playing at a gig, the phone rang, and after she quietly answered it, she dressed and left in her car. When she had not returned the next morning, I asked her boyfriend to help me find her. He drove me around the area where he knew she visited friends, but we did not find her car. I was gravely concerned and sensed that the situation was ominous. When she later showed up, she gave me no explanation for her absence, and I was left baffled. As these mysteries continued, nearing her ten years in the city, my husband encouraged me to bring her back to the old house. With his financial help, I rented a truck that Bret, the former military truck driver, was able to drive. Late one afternoon, with Dora's agreement, we drove to the city to meet her. Together, we packed all of her belongings and returned home. Following this episode, I made it clear that I would never again furnish an apartment for her out of town.

Dora was forced to live close to her ill brother, which was difficult. During the ensuing years, she made some attempts to relocate to the city when she occasionally held on to a job, but these were followed by returns home. During one attempt at city life again, I had her car repaired. It was disheartening when I learned that she had allowed a girlfriend to borrow the car, which she totaled and abandoned. It was the last time I gave Dora a car for city use. During this period, I learned that she was sleeping on the couch in an older man's apartment. This was a pattern that was repeated for a few years. Once Dora showed me pictures of a lovely condo she shared with a new male friend. Like so many of these arrangements, they did not last. Her brother, who had visited her at her last place, was appalled at a shouting incident she'd had in the street. This was typical of an inexplicable pattern of behavior we had not witnessed previously in her life.

One night she called me from a nearby town and explained that she was driving a getaway car for a collection agency. It was dangerous, she admitted. She was given room and board somewhere in the city in exchange for being available to drive nights when her boss was out on vehicle collections.

When my husband and I were in the city to attend the wedding of his eldest son, I sought to find Dora. I finally discovered her curled up on the couch of a girlfriend's apartment, totally uncommunicative. I could not get a word out of her and had to continue to the wedding without seeing her at all.

A more promising relationship developed when she moved to another city to live and work for a young single father. It seemed like a good situation for Dora if she could be responsible. The man had a business and owned a lovely mobile home in a gated community near the waterfront. Dora had to keep house and care for his darling little girl. My youngest daughter and I visited for one night and enjoyed the trip as Dora took pride in showing us around the place. Later that night, as I tried to sleep, I realized Dora was engaged in conversation with someone outside. For hours, the two female voices chattered fast and excitably, but I was unable to understand why they were so animated. It was years later, when I read about the effects of cocaine, that I surmised she must have been using drugs, which she obtained at the local marina bar. Inevitably the relationship was terminated, and the man brought her home to me.

Later in life, Dora confided in me about her ten-year use of cocaine. She explained her disappearance on the night I had visited her in the city as a call from friends using drugs. She related a dangerous experience she had when she joined them and started to have heart palpitations. Terrified, she screamed for them to call an ambulance that took her to an emergency room. By this time, she was angry with them for jeopardizing her health. For the rest of her life, she remained convinced that she had serious heart damage. Her later autopsy confirmed both heart and kidney damage from her lifestyle.

Dora returned to the old house and occupied the main area that was now separated from Bret's apartment. I had one experience where I had to walk away from her because she exhibited extreme anger under the influence of alcohol. There was no way to converse, and I left dismayed at seeing her beautiful face distorted with anger. This was not the daughter I loved and knew. I wondered how much of this inner hate was the result of her loss of the father she adored. I don't think she ever came to terms with his death when she was only ten years old.

While Dora remained stuck in a small town where there were few jobs, living adjacent to her mentally ill brother, my two younger children had completed junior college and moved on to careers in Hawaii at the marine base. I had completed my college degrees and occasionally took jobs between caring for my third husband, who was suffering from heart and cancer problems.

During a calmer period, I made a trip to Hawaii to visit my children. My youngest daughter had no problems finding jobs there—waitressing at the base and working as a travel agent and at a hospital. She had met a marine, and he asked her to care for his twin girls, whom he had custody of, while he was deployed to Iraq. For a young woman, just ten years their senior, I think she did an admirable job while working part-time and serving as a mother.

On the several trips I made to Hawaii, I was often left to entertain myself while the family worked. One day, while on the beach, I had a disturbing premonition that I should return home at once. I did not want to change plans, so with trepidation I telephoned Dora instead. I learned that she had been picked up for a DUI and would lose her license. Shaken and disappointed, I remained in Hawaii for the duration of the trip unaware of the turmoil Dora was experiencing. Later I found a suicide note she had written following this incident. Luckily Dora had met a young college student in a bar prior to the DUI, and he became her companion for the next several years. She later confided that she had wanted to commit suicide that weekend I called but was unable to carry it out. If she had owned a gun, I believe she would have ended her life then at thirty-one.

Following my return home, I began to hear about Dora's new friend, who had declared he would marry her. Rob bought an engagement diamond that she always wore until it was removed following her eventual funeral. He quickly changed Dora for the better. He let her know that he would not tolerate drugs or alcoholism. And for him she did change. He also influenced how she dressed and improved her makeup for the better. She soon stopped plucking her eyebrows into narrow lines and working hours on her mascara. Previously she had looked hard, but now she appeared more natural as she responded to someone she adored. She shared his college apartment much of the next few years and kept it clean and orderly in exchange for his companionship. Like many college students, Rob had a collection of exotic pets that were a challenge for Dora to care for. In the bathroom there was an iguana, and in the bedroom he kept a large boa constrictor. The snake presented a problem because the rabbits she loved, which Rob kept in cages, were fed to the snake. This Dora found so offensive that to save them she sometimes brought the rabbits to the old house and kept them on a screened back porch. I later found that the rabbits had chewed some of the wallboard in the room and that they had been attacked. At the house, Dora also had her own menagerie of cats, which were her babies. She mothered each of them and gave them special names like Rocky, Sasha, and Jasmine.

I felt that I now had another son when it came to Rob. One evening I was called to the scene of a car accident that Dora and Rob were involved in. An undocumented worker had run into Rob's car, which had stopped to make a turn. Rob was thrown from the vehicle, and Dora was traumatized, sitting in the front seat. The other driver fled the scene and ran into the woods. For the next few days, I had to drive Rob to take care of business related to the accident until he purchased a new car.

Rob frequently was at the old house when I visited. He would show up at the door wearing old, torn jeans, with a mop of unruly dark hair and bare feet. His clothes belied the fact that he was from a fine middle-class home. I think he was trying to fit in to his idea of the local college scene. I never saw him dressed up even when I took Dora and him to lunch. His was a difficult life at the time because his father, a West Point graduate, lay in a nursing home dying from exposure to Agent Orange.

I remained grateful for the positive changes Dora exhibited with Rob's help. However, I was not prepared for him training Dora to use guns. He took her to a local rifle range where he instructed her in shooting. I also found that he had signed her up with the NRA using my property as his address. He soon bought Dora several guns, explaining that he thought she needed protection against the friends Bret had about the premises. Dora had a small personal gun that she kept in her purse—the gun she eventually used to kill herself, which at the time was still listed as being owned by Rob.

Nearing his graduation, Rob took Dora to Las Vegas on a trip they taped together. This remains my only audio of Dora, although brief. The trip coincided with Rob preparing to leave town and return to his mother's home until he found a job. Rob was moving on with his life, and Dora did not comprehend it. She was several years his senior, and his mother had not accepted her after they met. Later Rob moved out of the state, found a career in social work, rejected Dora, and finally married another girl. It was at his apartment that Dora died.

7

There's Been a Tragedy

May 28 started as a hectic day for me as I worked to finish moving from the townhouse I had shared with my late husband to the old house a block away. Since the death of my husband and Dora's move, I was now alone with Bret. As I carried boxes in and dropped them on the floor, I wished I had time to rake the yard where the tall pine trees were swaying in the wind along a brook winding across our one and a third acres of land. I had been forced to sell the townhouse, which would not accept Bret, and move into the property I had purchased to protect him. My late husband had warned me that keeping up two residences was not feasible, and therefore, I had no recourse. I had helped Dora move to another state, where she hoped to rekindle a relationship with her boyfriend of six years. She still wore the diamond ring he had given her soon after they met, but he had never made it clear where their relationship was going when he moved away.

At the beginning of the week, I called Dora twice regarding her cat, which she had left behind when she moved. Earlier she had expressed interest in finding a home for Jasmine, and I thought I had made a good decision when a nurse took the pet. However, she was upset with me, which regretfully turned out to be my last conversation with her.

Ten days prior, I had flown to visit her after a trip to see my pregnant daughter. Dora had proudly shown me around the city she had adopted. In her few months there, she had made friends, found an apartment, and was starting her second job. We had shopped for some items for her studio apartment. Since she had been sleeping on the floor, I purchased a futon and some small tables. Her refrigerator was well stocked with food for which I was grateful. I found that in the local heat she could not afford to run the air conditioner, and I wondered how she could have taken care of her prize cat under these conditions.

During this last visit with Dora, we had lunch with a lovely cousin of mine who spent winters in the area. Dora seemed elated and filled with enthusiasm about her new life, and I detected no signs of despair. She had the new small car I had purchased for her, and she had met me at the airport; I can still see her beaming at the bottom of the escalator as I arrived. When I departed, we said goodbye in the parking lot of the airport, and I felt confident about her move and her future. She seemed to be in one of her upbeat periods.

It was only ten days after I returned home, amid the turmoil of the move, that I received an early evening call. "This is the police department," a voice said. "There has been a tragedy," he continued. "Dora?" I asked. "She has been shot," he said. "Where is she?" I pleaded with impending shock beginning to consume me. He continued methodically on script, trying to break terrible news to a mother. "She was taken to the hospital," he answered, "and she won't make it." After a pause, he admitted that she was now at the coroner's office. "Are you alone?" he asked. Slumping to the floor, I responded, "Yes." In my confusion and utter disbelief, I recall him asking whom he could call for me. I explained that I was in the middle of moving and had no idea where my phone or address books were. All I could feel was a sense of unreality; these things only happen to other people, or in movies, or on the soap operas Dora loved to watch. I mumbled that my youngest son was in the marines somewhere on the East Coast. But the efficient officer had more questions on his list. "Do you want her gun returned?" "No, no!" With his continuing insistence that he wanted to call someone for me, I could only think of my pastor. I mentioned his name and my church, but I did not have a number then. My closest friends were out of town, my family was far away, and I was in the process of moving. I didn't ask about the tragic details but left that to my younger marine son to learn. Intuitively I knew that Dora must have shot herself, and I never asked. I couldn't fathom any other episode at the time, but why? It was so soon after our wonderful, promising visit. The rest of the evening was a blur. I must have made some wrenching phone calls to a brother, for members of his family soon arrived and tried to console me.

I only remember sitting on a kitchen stool for the next few hours. My pastor came, but a relative must have taken over and convinced him that they were caring for me. A niece went to Bret's apartment and told him the news. I did not confront him that evening. His reaction was intuitive as he stated that she should never have had a gun. That night I was taken to a relative's home to try to sleep. Meanwhile, the police officer, at my request, had made a call to my youngest daughter who was pregnant with her second child. Fortunately, she had her twin stepdaughters with her while her husband was away on duty. Because of her condition, I urged her not to make a flight to be with me. She sent flowers addressed to "sister and aunt." By the following day, the Red Cross had located my military son and his wife. When informed of the tragedy, he was released to grieve and take over some duties for me. He flew to her new home where he met with the police, detectives, the boyfriend, her employer, her apartment manager, etc. Until his trip I had none of the details except that she was shot and deceased. Not much more mattered now that I would no longer have her alive.

The drama concerning her death that I later learned about was more upsetting than I could have imagined. On her last day, she had dressed for work but first went to confront her boyfriend at his apartment. What was said I don't know, but she returned to her apartment, wrote a suicide note that was later found by the police, picked up her gun, and returned to her former lover's apartment. There she pointed the gun at him and reminded him that he had bought it for her and taught her to use it. He was helpless to reach a phone or to stop her. She only said, "You have broken my heart, now I am going to break yours." She then shot herself in the heart and died instantly.

When my son met with the former boyfriend, his mother had arrived and expressed her condolences. She stated that they were not to blame. Blame was not something I dwelled on. Instead I was just grateful that in her warped sense of despair, she had not shot her boyfriend. He did not attend Dora's funeral, nor have we had any contact since. He subsequently married.

I can only dwell on the six happy years that Dora and he shared when they were committed to each other. They had been inseparable while he attended the local college. The then tall, lanky, often barefoot student had spent time at our house. He had become a part of our lives.

During the next few days, I went about the terrible experience of getting my daughter's body back as I planned a funeral alone. My younger son arrived after closing her apartment and stopping to visit his sister. One of my brothers flew in while another brother helped briefly. I met with my pastor and arranged for a small service. The suicide note found in Dora's apartment was returned to me. It read, "Rob was my future. There is nothing to live for anymore." On the back she had written, "I'm sorry."

When my son arrived with Dora's belongings in her car, I put her things away. Later I found her diaries and a collection of poems. I have included some of her poems and remarks later in this book because they help to illustrate her frame of mind at the time. She wrote, "I'm thirty-seven now and still feel like I'm twenty-five. I feel my looks are improving with age so I don't mind getting older. I never thought I'd make it this far in age. Sometimes I surprise myself."

Following a small funeral, cremation, and burial in a family plot, my marine son had to return to duty across the country. Death was not foreign to either of us. His father died when he was barely four years old, and he only had vague memories of his dad in a nursing home. In later years, I had lost both of my parents. There were the two deaths of cousins in town, and my husband, who had provided the home where my children grew up, succumbed to cancer. My son and son-in-law had stood at his funeral in their marine uniforms. But I learned that there is nothing to prepare a parent for the death of a child at any age. Dora was almost thirty-nine and died the same summer as Princess Diana, whom I admired. The years have never stopped me from missing Dora's presence and her ups and downs.

Life at the old house has sheltered many tragedies for me. I watched as my son battled schizophrenia and alcoholism. My late husband died of cancer. My younger son was deployed to Iraq three times, and his best friend was killed on his motorcycle outside of our town. Happily, my late husband's family grew to nine grandchildren. Years earlier, when my first husband died, I prayed that I never would become bitter. I had an elderly, wealthy relative, who sometimes called and took me to lunch before her death. She had read the book *The Art of Selfishness* and recommended it to me. I felt that despite all of her money and an apartment on Nob Hill in San Francisco, she had found no happiness but just bitterness. I vowed never to be like her.

Unlike the aftermath of my first husband's death, this time I sought help. I joined a small hospice group and had plenty of friendships. For a time I dated a gentleman who helped me with my computer and printer and took me on trips to interesting places in our state. We also joined a group that toured Alaska for a week. He was available for some time before I moved on. Another social event was a regular meeting of singles at a local restaurant, which became an outlet for meeting people. There I also met a gentleman who wanted to become involved in a relationship, but I was not ready. Following my last marriage, I had quite high standards for a spouse.

A friend had suggested a counselor after Dora's death, and she was most helpful. With her expertise, it became clearer to me that Dora had been a victim of more than depression. Through my studies, I concluded that Dora had suffered from moderate personality disorder and was bipolar. I was aware that Dora had overcome many obstacles—dyslexia, bulimia, depression, drug abuse, and alcoholism. Most of all, Dora mourned her late father. My only solace was in her love for and appreciation of me. I hoped I had never let her down. There are no regrets for reaching out to her and caring for her when she was down. I found a poem she wrote, and as with other poems, I have included them for their content rather than for style. They illustrate her state of mind far better than anything I could write, so consider her thoughts with an open mind.

My Sweet Mother

I want you to know
My sweet mother
That I thank you every day
For all you do for me.
Keep your spirits up
Because you have us
Standing by you always.
I appreciate all the things
You do even though you
Might not think I do.
We kids would be lost without
Your guidance and love.
But you are still here, and
You will live a long, happy life
With tons of love coming your way,
Thank you, Mother, for all you do.
Dora

Excerpts from the Diaries

Among my daughter's belongings, I found a box of diaries that she had kept from the day she met her boyfriend, Rob. They were intended to be private, but they ended up in my possession. Most of the entries were intimate and meant to be destroyed, but since there were often references to the times I spent with her, I was reluctant to let go of them. However, after several years, I selected parts that related to her thinking and moods, and copied them, but I destroyed the private comments. As I ripped each page of her diary, I felt that I was letting her go at last. It was what she clearly would have wanted, and I hoped I did not betray her trust by hanging on to them so long.

Once, when Dora was living with me, I noticed that she was writing, and I asked what she was doing. She quickly replied that she was writing poetry, but she did not suggest that I read it. Since I always respected the privacy of my children, I never read her poems, mail, or diaries until some were returned to me. If she wanted to share them with me, she could have done so while alive. In sharing selected pieces, I have often had to modify her language for printing. She had moments when she expressed immense anger by swearing. If she had been drinking, I couldn't talk to her or share what she was thinking. When cross, her mouth would twist into a snarl, and she could be unpleasant. Thankfully, these times were few and infrequent. I saw less as she matured.

During the seven years that I cared for her as an adult, we often spent time shopping at the mall, having lunch at a bistro, or sharing coffee from the cappuccino machine I had purchased for her. She had no problem operating the machine, but I always had to call her for directions, which I think amused her. We seemed to have an affable relationship while she lived near me. Our only disagreements concerned my care of her ill elder brother. She resented the people who congregated with Bret under the mulberry tree. She was appalled when I purchased a motorcycle for Bret and rightfully so; it was during one of my weaker moments. She disliked Bret's dog, and he reciprocated with distaste of her cats. For some reason, she also disliked my poodle. I almost felt that she was jealous of my pet.

The diaries chronicle the seven years she was in a relationship with Rob, during his college years and then the several years of separation when he moved on. She also had kept the numerous poems Rob had written to her, but as lovely as they are, I can't legally publish them. Most of her remaining years were spent living in the old house, separate from but still close to Bret. She had often spent time with him at his apartment near the college. Although Rob had given Dora an engagement ring and confessed continuing love for her, he was not destined to marry her. He was several years younger than her and an only child. Rob was expected to have an heir, and Dora, by her own volition, had had her tubes tied at twenty-one. She felt she could never be adequate as a mother perhaps because she realized what demons she was dealing with. She wrote once that she never wanted to have a life of struggles like she saw in mine. The slow death of her father and my brief unhappy remarriage turned her against bringing children into the world as she saw it. Following Dora's tragic death at Rob's apartment, he did move on; he married and raised a daughter.

The excerpts from Dora's writings chronicle the ebbs and flows of a deep love affair between two young people. I decided some were relevant because they present a window into the thinking and emotions of one who was suffering great pain and anguish, one who was probably ill. Earlier, after receiving a love poem from Rob, Dora wrote, "I'm in my messed-up mood swing again; part of the day I'm feeling fine, and another part I'm fantasizing about killing myself. I get angrier as the days go by. Depression wants me to drown in it. No wonder nobody wants to be around me. I'm just a barrel of laughs these days. God should have taken me instead of my dad. My dad was so kindhearted and such a good person."

The aftermath of sharing a house with her ill brother prompted many excerpts. On one occasion, she wrote, "Had a terrible nightmare last night, and Bret's friend caused it. I tried to have Bret arrested this afternoon but to no avail. He has to attack me before that happens. I can't stand this anymore. I am so miserable right now that I just want to end my life. I can't stand this world any longer. When my time is up, it's going to be a celebration FOREVER."

Again she cried out, "Woke up and got real depressed. I cried a little. I can't wait to be away from Bret and live somewhere else far, far away. If Mom knew what is good for her, she too would have him put somewhere else under lock and key so that he won't hassle her anymore. God, please sell this house so I can start a new, fresh life somewhere else. My mother also deserves much better."

Unfortunately, Dora and I were victims of a social system that has abandoned the mentally ill and placed all of the responsibility on the family. These excerpts are a small illustration of what the family had been relegated to care for. With the closure of hospitals for the mentally ill, families now carry the burden of care alone. I never once had anyone intervene or offer a break from the daily care of my son. With the abolishment of state hospital systems, it was expected that the states would pick up the care of the ill, but this never happened and probably never will.

At other times, Dora tried to find purpose in her life. In 1994, she wrote, "I have been doing some soul-searching this morning, and have come to the conclusion that since my boyfriend is leaving college in two months, God's plans for me now are to help my mother out with the house. There is yard work to do and plants to water. Bret needs keeping an eye on, and there are the cats to care for. Also, we need to make sure we don't get ripped off again. I gave Rob all of me for several years—washed his clothes, cleaned his apartment, cooked for him, gave him moral support, and more. Now it is time to help my mom out since she is helping with a roof over my head. Hopefully I can get work soon. This is God's plan for me now. And Rob and I will always be close friends and lovers if we both want it to stay that way: I do forever; I'll always love Rob."

For a time, Dora did leave the house and move to the nearby university town. There she got a job and an apartment, which she decorated with her inimitable touch in the hope that Rob would at least visit her for Christmas. When this did not happen, she moved into my townhouse while she sorted out her life. My younger daughter and her baby had spent five months there with me while her husband was in training elsewhere. With a room now available, Dora moved in until her eventual move out of state.

As she sorted out her plans, Dora made a list of goals for herself:

1. Have patience.
2. Have faith in God.
3. Have trust.
4. Thank God for the gifts you do have.
5. Take one day at a time.
6. Be happy and appreciate life in the here and now.
7. Don't worry so much about things that will never happen.
8. Be kind and generous.
9. Appreciate what you have.
10. Enjoy life to the fullest now for the short time we are here on earth.
11. God is guiding your life so have faith and patience.
12. Remember, everything happens for a reason.

Again she wrote, "I never thought I'd make it this far in age. Sometimes I surprise myself."

Always obsessed with her appearance, she wrote, "I'm a happy camper right now. I weighed in at 104 pounds this morning, and that's my ideal weight, just what I want to be. Now, to keep it there is the hard part." This went back to her teen years when she suddenly lost weight. She later admitted to me that she had bulimia for several years.

July 26: "I am off probation today. Yah! I think I'll fix myself a drink since I am the only one to celebrate with myself. Me, myself, and Jasmine, my sweet cat, that's all I'll ever have. Mom has her own life with her friends, and Rob is ready to leave me. That's the story of my life. Nobody wants me."

Dec. 3, 1996: "I'm getting ready for work and thinking about my new plan for 1997. No matter what happens with Rob and me, I will plan on moving in the middle of May to find a place to live. Nothing is going to stand in my way, and that is a promise I've made. I'm strong, and I will start a new life for myself this summer, full speed ahead!"

1994: "I wish I knew where my life is going to end up, with Rob or with someone else, or just by myself. It's scary for me too. I have a beautiful house to live in for now, and I will help my mom out for now and be there for her, so for now that is my duty."

"I was in one of my self-pity, depressing moods about having no friends here to do things with. Things have to change soon before I have a nervous breakdown and do something I regret."

1997: "I am not going to feel weak and helpless with no control over my actions. I am in control with God's help and his son, Jesus Christ, and my dear father, who are with me at all times and guiding my life to a wonderful future. I don't need anyone. I can make it just fine on my own, and I will!"

Her last note before committing suicide said, "Rob was my future. There is nothing to live for anymore. I'm sorry, Dora."

I hope sharing these thoughts will help someone else who is facing a drama like mine, or perhaps a student studying in the field of mental illness will learn from these writings. I have kept these stories for close to twenty years now, and if they are to be shared, it is now. As a mother, I can say that losing a child leaves a hole so large that nothing can fill it again. Thoughts of the loved one never leave for a week, a day, or an hour. I have had the fortune to survive and remarry. Although my days are still filled with heartache, I have others to consider and live for.

8

Saying Goodbye

Following the funeral, I was left with the old house to organize. Unopened boxes remained piled on the floor. A brother, who was visiting, slept on an unassembled bed mattress on the floor. Prior to the funeral, my moving had come to a halt. No one had thought to open boxes or assemble a bed. Once my relatives, including my marine son and his wife, had departed, I faced the task of arranging the house as best I could after leaving the townhouse. The old place began to grow on me as memories of Dora remained. The sixties style of flooring and pine-paneled walls took on a quaint charm. And there were always the woods behind and the weeds to tend. However, for the first time, I was now living in close proximity to Bret, and I experienced some of the frustrating problems that Dora had endured during the years she lived there alone. Bret was a constant annoyance, causing interruptions, playing loud music, banging on the walls, and drinking until he collapsed.

Gratefully I had memories of the recent visit with Dora. I recalled her excitement about her new job as a cocktail waitress. Years earlier, I had paid for her to take the bartenders course she wanted. She was proud of her independence and the ability to use her skills. It was probably not the best place for someone who could abuse alcohol, but she liked the atmosphere of music and people. She was also proud that she had qualified for an apartment on her own, and she was dating and making friends. However, underneath it all, she was not coping with Rob's rejection. I later learned that she often sat in her car at his apartment hoping to catch a glimpse of him. Sadly, I learned that Rob had advised another girlfriend he had to stay away from his place because he questioned Dora's behavior. Little did any of us know that Dora had but ten days to live when I last saw her.

I was haunted by my last telephone conversation with her when, after accusations of favoritism about the cats, I had hung up. During the next few days, I had a premonition that I should call back, but I neglected to act on it. She had a call system for only local calls, so I had to call. Being in the middle of a move at the time, I could not cope with irrational thinking. I had struggled for days to call but turned to immediate duties first. Dora had thought about suicide all of her life, and I doubt I could have stopped her. The fact was Dora wanted to be with her deceased father, whom she worshipped. I often despair about what he would have had to bear had he lived and known of her problems. At times I would feel as though I had let him down. Certainly, if he had lived, I think I would still have Dora. Often I tremble with despair should their father know of the condition Bret lives in. If there is a heaven, I hope my first husband has been spared the misery I have endured in raising our two eldest children. On the other hand, I often wish he could know the success of our two youngest children.

From comments made by the detective on her case, I realized the police had read some of the last excerpts from Dora's diary because they mentioned my conversation with her about the cat. However, when they found my check to Dora for rent money pinned to the wall and read further in the diary, they realized I had done all I could. I saw Dora's behavior her last few days as a moment of paranoia after a bout with drinking gave her alcohol poisoning that last week. How I wish our last words had been more understanding, but life does not give us a second opportunity. Both Rob, because Dora's gun was registered to him, and I were briefly questioned about her death but quickly cleared when the authorities read her diary.

I recalled the last words I'd had at her father's bedside before he expired. He had inquired about how we would cope financially since we had no life insurance. I assured him that we would continue as we were, but with Social Security benefits while I continued college studies to achieve my dream of being a teacher. Then I said, "Thank you for the children." They are my jewels from a tragedy.

And there were the last words with my third husband as he was rolled into a nursing home on a stretcher. He complained about terrible pain first. Knowing his concern about finances, I assured him that he had three weeks of coverage. Then I looked at him and said, "You have been a good husband," to which he shook his head in disagreement. Soon he was sedated, free from pain, and in a coma with nothing more to be said. I could only sit by his bedside and wait for the end.

My last walk with my dying father was kind and understanding. I confided, "Dad, I can't get along with Mother!" He replied, "Doll, no one can get along with her." What a comfort for me to be assured that I was not alone or responsible for a very contentious relationship with my mother.

Following my father's funeral, the family had gathered at my mother's townhouse. There was some unleashing of tensions as Mother jested, trying on some of Dad's hats. While some great pictures were taken, they were lost forever when my middle brother took them home and forgot to empty his pockets before washing his clothes, which ruined the film— not unexpected of my brother. At my father's funeral, it was confirmed that we had a half brother whose existence had been carefully hidden from us. It had been a skeleton in our closet for years. Also, following the funeral, I was shown an insurance policy for the first time that my father had taken out after my birth. Confusion arose over the wording because it was made out to my mother and me. The word *and* instead of *or* meant that I was half owner. One of my brothers showed it to me and asked if I knew about it. Surprised at seeing it, I told the family I had never been aware of it. Not long afterward, I flew home. I received a call from the insurance company days later saying that my mother was trying to cash in the insurance and was upset that she had to have my signature on it. Mother later called and insisted that I must sign the papers. With four children to care for, I said nothing to her and cashed my share when I received the forms. She had kept the policy hidden from me for sixty years.

Dora's funeral had been well attended considering how few friends she had. A girlfriend had driven four hours to be there, along with many relatives from her father's side. Her friend gave me a copy of a letter she had received from Dora telling her about her new life. She felt that Dora was lonely and had always been looking for a permanent relationship, for someone she could depend on with unconditional love like the relationship with her late father.

In the following months, I had time to glance through Dora's poems and diaries. There was much to surprise me but more I'd prefer not to know. The diaries were intimate reminders of her life with Rob with whom she had left them before she shot herself. For some years, I could not part with them, but I let them go as earlier described.

I had much to do at the time because I remained Bret's only caretaker and settled close to him. There, I resumed my hobby of quilting, which had become somewhat of a career for me. Eventually, as I grieved, I made a large quilt commemorating my two eldest children. It relates their life and illness; it is in their memory and has been shared in quilt shows.

The quilt is called "My Son, My Daughter, A Journal of Mental Illness." Twelve blocks depict the lives of both children. Later I had a booklet published with directions for the project. The quilt also won awards and was published in a magazine.

At a later time, I made a wall hanging commemorating Dora done in circles as a guild project. During my father's declining years, he devoted his time to a large family tree that compiled our history back to the 1300s in France. He had large copies printed for the family. I have mine framed and hanging in my entry. It is a wonderful piece of his life, and I would like to emulate his gift with my art pieces.

The ensuing years at the house kept me occupied—renovating, caring for Bret, and trying to move on from grief. Bret continued to drink so I could not take him out socially. I had friends from hospice visit and even took trips with some. Our group held monthly potlucks and helped us all through our immediate grief.

A church friend invited me to a scrapbooking class where I constructed a memory book of Dora. It culminated in a lovely tribute to her life, and I keep it close on the coffee table. While I still grieve, her two younger siblings have moved on with productive lives: my son in the military, and my daughter, a mother and schoolteacher. Since they were much younger and had experienced lives that were different from their older siblings, they did not seem to share the grief I felt.

Again my friend from church suggested I go to counseling, where I had to confront post-traumatic stress disorder. The telephone call from the police about Dora's death continued to haunt me like a recording in my mind. Only time would help me with the pain.

Through hospice I had made friends and enjoyed a social life, but there was no end to problems with Bret, as his friends kept drinking with him under the mulberry tree. The police checked in when there were occasional complaints. I had lost control. I could no longer take trips and cruises as I had enjoyed when Dora watched the house and Bret. Instead I enrolled in computer classes at the college and the high school and tried to upgrade my skills. A friend helped me out with new techniques and shared CDs with me. I was able to entertain visitors at times; a stepdaughter visited for ten days. When my daughter's stepdaughter had a baby in the town near me, I was called to her emergency delivery on the Fourth of July because the family could not get there in time. The baby was handed to me to hold after delivery. Following the birth of the tiny girl, the new mother and her twin sister stayed at my house.

For years, a stepson visited twice a year with his two daughters. For them, I was the only grandma left. They would come for their summer visit and then announce that they could come for Thanksgiving. We spent our time looking for Beanie Babies. I have been privileged to see these young people grow into adulthood, graduate from college, honor our country with military service, and marry. They are such a pride and joy.

My military son was back and forth and eventually introduced me to his future wife from Norway. My son had seen me through many tragedies while I owned the house. I had attended the funerals of too many in our family. I depended on him to keep me updated with purchases of computer equipment.

Now I had my birds, dog, and cats to keep me company. I never felt alone as I pursued various hobbies and learned new skills. My son maintains that he could see a change in my demeanor when I later met my fourth husband and married again. If I felt alone, I was just adjusting to tragedy. Every Saturday I made a batch of cookies that I took on Sunday to church, where I was responsible for the coffee hour. I enjoyed this opportunity to serve with little fanfare. I also ushered and played in the bell choir.

At the time, I saw no future for me other than living in the old house and caring for Bret. I dreamed of writing more quilt books, but I had little strength left to finish a big project. I started writing these memories of life with Dora, which took years to put into book form. Perhaps coping with one day at a time was the best I could do under the circumstances. I allowed the old house to become a refuge as I healed and accepted the reality of what I had faced. Unbeknown to me then, I would later move and let go of my son. The house was situated on a busy main street with a public building on one side, a brook and a hill on the other side, and woods in back. With the separation, I had no neighbors, and the tragedies that played out in my life there were my own. If I ever heard from a distant neighbor, it was to complain about Bret. I was truly isolated and left in my own vacuum to survive. Later, when I moved to a large city, I attended a big church and realized that I was alone with my scars. The preacher had no idea who I was, and when I moved, I was surely never missed. Only a wonderful assistant pastor has kept up with me. In contrast, my mother would make herself known quickly wherever she went. She became indispensable. In my shyness, and with my life's tragedies, I felt I was only a spoke in a wheel, someone drifting. It has only been through my published works that I have felt I had an identity. I do not want to be stoic, but it helps to share and to be appreciated for surviving. Perhaps this is why I burden myself with writing about my life experiences.

9

Letting Go

While out shopping one day, I made an impulsive decision to visit a Realtor friend. I had not thought of moving from the old house, but here I was, talking to her about selling the place. Within an hour I had listed my home, which had been my only place to house Bret. For eighteen years, I had struggled to pay the mortgage and maintain the premises. Truthfully, I never thought it would sell so I was shocked when, within four days, I had a buyer. With no backup plan, I suddenly had to leave the place in three weeks. It was my daughter and her family who pitched in and made decisions for me. They arranged a truck rental, packed it, and moved my furniture into storage while I temporarily lived with them.

In retrospect, maybe I had just reached my rope's end taking care of the house and Bret. After all these years, I had made no progress in helping my son. He still sat under the mulberry tree and lined up the beer cans on the windowsill. Now, without my husband or eldest daughter, perhaps I needed a different perspective on life.

The first problem was what to do with Bret. He challenged me about letting him go. "Is this what you really want?" he said. He questioned whether I could let go of his sanctuary after all these years. It took police intervention to calm him, and they decided to move him to a halfway house in the next town. The occupants were recent parolees from jail and not necessarily mentally ill. They shared an old house in the woods and cooked their own meals. The occupants spent most days attending church services at a small edifice nearby. On several occasions, I attended the services to see what Bret was confronting in his new place. There was no sermon; instead the congregation sang or marched around the room. At times, when someone fell in a trance, the person would be caught and led back into the line of marchers. The owner would show up in a Cadillac or on a Harley Davidson motorcycle, on which he later died in an accident. He seemed well compensated for his enterprise. However, the men and women attending had few options. It was either this or the streets because our system has few choices for the homeless.

With the help of my family, my move was quickly accomplished. In the confusion, my pets were frightened and disappeared, except for my dog. When it came time to leave, my dog was put in my car, but the birds had to be left behind, and the cats could not be found. All I could do was leave them for the new occupants to care for. My poor cat, Minny, was later found behind the stove, and the new owners found homes for the pets. My daughter had her own menagerie of pets and could not take any more.

At my daughter's house, I shared a room with my young granddaughter. I frequently called Bret and heard of no serious problems. He had taken his dog with him, but I doubt money was available to feed it. Bret did not complain, and I decided to enjoy my life. During my stay at my daughter's house, I flew to Europe to attend my son's wedding. It was held in the ornate church that his paternal grandparents had attended until they immigrated to Canada. Soon after my return, my daughter found an apartment for me, and we emptied the storage unit so I could live on my own again.

After Bret had been living separated from me for six months, I decided to visit him for his birthday. I bought him a large cake to share with all of the occupants and drove the ten hours north, where I booked a hotel. However, my plans were smashed when I presented the cake and the director informed me that Bret had to leave immediately. That evening, I returned to my hotel room with Bret, and he had to sleep on the floor. There, friends of mine from hospice days knocked on my door to say hello. The next morning, I had no option but to resume my trip back home, where I again had to take care of Bret. In the confusion, I did not know what happened to his dog. My lease would not have allowed a dog anyway.

Shortly after Bret moved in with me, I realized that he had found a source of alcohol and was drinking. I now had control of his benefits check, but somehow he located money to purchase drinks. He soon came to the attention of the local police and a team called PERT (psychiatric emergency response team). They regularly checked on my welfare. Bret stayed with me for six difficult months before he was taken away. During that time, he found his way to the local shopping center where he somehow had money to buy liquor. Then he would hide in some abandoned fields among the weeds and drink. I spoke to the market manager, who immediately recognized my description of Bret. However, he could not prevent purchases of alcohol. Bret also had discovered a distant bar and made some commotion there. Again I seemed to be rescuing him often. When his condition became dire, he was taken to the local emergency room to dry out. Meanwhile, I had found a mental health-care provider, but still there was little support available except an occasional drying-out in the local jail. The agency later dropped him as a client because he did not cooperate.

PERT started making regular visits to my apartment. One day, when they dropped by, Bret was drunk and lying on the floor laughing deliriously. By now, he had been through the mental health system, treated often at the ER, and had been in and out of jail. The team eventually decided that I could not care for my son anymore. He was a tall, heavy fellow twice my size, and I was not equipped to handle him. Ultimately, the police became involved again, and Bret was removed from my home. Not long after he was taken, he telephoned from a restaurant and pleaded with me to pick him up. He had been left on the street downtown with no money or clothes. Perplexed, I considered my options, torn between picking him up and waiting for something else to happen. Eventually there was another call, and I learned that he was being taken to a care home. I wondered if he was being admitted to a facility because he was mentally ill and homeless. Had the police dropped him off to fulfill some protocol on placing him? Only the homeless ill are sometimes given housing. Following the break with Bret, I was advised of his address. It turned out to be a local, well-run, and clean private home not far away. He had to share a room, which was always difficult for him, and he was required to stop drinking and abide by the house regulations. A competent supervisor attended at all times. This was unlike most care homes I had observed so far.

His stay at the home didn't last long because he somehow managed to drink. This loss of a place repeated itself several times. We would find a place that was decent, and he would last there just days. We also became acquainted with a local hospital equipped with a locked floor that enabled people like Bret to spend time there to dry out. It was run by a church and was an excellent place to leave Bret if he would cooperate. Eventually he refused these services, and I had no backup place for him. He was also given the opportunity for daycare if he would cooperate, but this he refused as well. Bret continued to find excuses for his noncompliance with opportunities to get help. Often what held him back was his inability to be around others and to express himself verbally.

After months of trials in various care homes, Bret ended up living in an unsupervised private home considered to be independent living. Many similar places existed in the area for people who were simply trying to make a living. Those lucky enough to get a room had to adjust to a diet with lots of rice and beans.

Eventually Bret found a room where he resided for several years with both male and female residents. I became acquainted with the owner who lived in the garage. Most of the women lived upstairs, and the males shared rooms downstairs. They had a lovely view of downtown from the patio. Since Bret liked to cook, he often helped with the meals. Over the years, I continued to take an interest in the home and found the owner pleasant and friendly. While there, Bret became involved with a female resident with whom he spent the next several years. She had the remnants of a once-attractive face. However, she appeared ravaged by drug use like we saw in the sixties. Behind the pathetic façade were traces of beauty, blond hair, blue eyes, and a pleasant, once-tall physique now dressed inappropriately; her smile revealed many missing teeth. Her family had long given up caring for her, and she taught Bret how she had learned to survive. For one thing, this consisted of panhandling. She left every day for what she described as a church downtown. There she was given food and clothes and left to panhandle. I saw her as a survivor.

Some years later, a female resident attacked the owner of the home. The petite owner tried to defend herself, but when the police arrived, she was removed from her facility and taken to jail. Her boyfriend soon took her into his home with the understanding that she would never reside at her facility. She turned the operation over to her daughter, who employed jail parolees to run the place. Things quickly deteriorated, and I realized they were stealing the mail and perhaps other items. Some people died from drug overdoses, which brought the home to the attention of the authorities. Soon the place was closed, and the county sued the owners.

In the midst of the turmoil, Bret and his girlfriend found a room in the same neighborhood where they lived for some years until the girl took off with another man. This devastated Bret, who truly loved the girl. He mourned her loss for months. Meanwhile he was moved to a single room in the house. As of this writing, Bret has remained in the same home for close to ten years. The girlfriend tried to return but was never allowed to live there again because of her drug use. The owners keep Bret because they know he is not dangerous, and they tolerate his drinking. Doctors regularly visit the clients.

When I visited, Bret had a bed, a dresser, and a fan. Once I learned that he had been beaten up on the street, but Bret took responsibility for it saying it was his fault. I was also informed that he was once hospitalized after collapsing on the street. I wish I had been informed of these incidents, but Bret is independent, and I have filed no papers for guardianship. What could I do anyway?

During this period, my visits often upset Bret. One day I searched and located him drinking behind a local market. He became angry with me and asked me to leave him alone. I had recently moved from my condo to a retirement apartment. There I made many friends, in particular a couple upstairs in my building. One day, as I stood outside talking to neighbors, I learned that the wife in that couple had died. Suddenly the neighbor appeared, and we embraced him, offering our condolences. Many of the neighbors pitched in to help with a luncheon following her memorial service, to which the widower drove me.

Following his wife's funeral, the man started inviting me to his place for dinner. This continued through the summer until my younger son and daughter-in-law wanted me to move east. Both of my military families were being transferred—my youngest son and his wife retiring to Europe, and my daughter and her family to the East Coast. Before I could assimilate the impact on my life, my younger son had purchased a condo for me so I could live near my daughter and her family. I now faced leaving Bret on his own and saying what I thought would be a farewell forever to my widower friend.

All too soon a truck was at my place to move me. I said goodbye to Bret and waited at my friend's apartment for my younger son to pick me up. I was in a daze and unable to comprehend what or why this was happening to me. Somehow I was being thrown into a whole new situation beyond my control. Neither my friend nor I could see the future. I could not think of being without him, yet here I was moving on again. During the winter months, I had occasions to return and visit my friend, who now expressed sincere interest in a permanent relationship. Twice I visited him for several weeks—first when he had surgery and again when he took me to his time-share for a vacation. Both times I checked in on Bret, who still lived with his girlfriend.

Within the year, I again visited my friend who had decided to move to Florida to live with a daughter. From there he made trips to Virginia to spend time with me. On my eightieth birthday, we quietly married at my daughter's house. My son and his family later came from Europe and treated us to a celebration in New York City. At my request, we had dinner downtown at Fraunces Tavern, which is the historical home of my ancestors. We saw a show and where the Twin Towers had fallen, enjoying the start of a new life. My husband had sold all of his furniture and moved in with me, along with his truckload of books. Eventually we moved midway south, where we were seven hours from his girls in Florida and seven hours from my daughter in Virginia. I worry about Bret every day but realize now that I can do nothing for him. The whole system has let him down. I keep in touch by cell phone and send gift certificates.

Since my last visit, I purchased a small cooler for food and sent several food packages. The future is unknown for us. I miss my son and now require medication to control my grief. If only he could respond to medication as my uncle did years ago. What potential could he have? My youngest son visits me from Europe on business trips, and I see an uncanny resemblance to Bret in his hazel eyes. If only Bret could achieve what my other son has. Why have two children been so productive while two fell through the cracks? Do skeletons from the closet have the answer? Is there anything I missed, or was it environment? It appears to be just genetic. Two sons with the same father but there is such a difference in them. One daughter is gone while the other is delightful and talented. I can find no answer and hope someday genetics will give us an explanation.

10
Guns

As a child, I played with neighbor friends whose father had a room devoted to a display of guns. The collection made no impression on me, except it seemed like a strange way to utilize an entire room. Years later I learned that the man had a fatal episode with the police when he became irrational and brandished a gun. Strangely, under stress, he collapsed and died without a gunshot on either side. Several years after that, I was advised that his eldest daughter committed suicide with a gun.

Later in my life, there was a tragedy involving two young men who lived next door to us. They walked into the woods holding their guns pointed downward in proper positions. However, one of the boys tripped, and his gun fired and killed his friend. Rumors and suspicions circulated, and the surviving young man quit school and joined the army.

My daughter owned guns. Her boyfriend bought her various types of guns for some misconceived notion that she needed protection from the friends of her mentally ill brother. He enrolled her in the NRA and taught her to fire the weapons. I was naive enough to dismiss the situation as the activities of two young college students. I never wanted to see the guns and left them to their own activities. One day, when Dora missed Rob, she said that she was suicidal. She had been in her bedroom writing poems to him, and I thought of the incident as a passing phase. She went for a walk and later returned with no further discussion. Like many other times, I should have taken her more seriously. Dora had a gun and could have used it at any time when she was despondent.

I never wanted to see my daughter's guns. I was terrified of them and believed I could never kill another human being or creature. When Dora decided to move, however, I was almost relieved that she had a gun under her seat in the car. She had a long, lonely trip through the desert, and I knew she could defend herself if necessary.

When I was notified that she had been shot, I was in shock. I instinctively suspected that Dora had shot herself before the police told me so. The officer had asked me if I wanted her gun. I suppose it was protocol to ask, but why would a mother want the gun that her daughter used to take her life? Horrified, I resolutely said, "No." I never saw her guns, and I never wanted to see them.

We hear much these days of the wrong people having guns, and I agree. Even Bret in his misery from mental illness realized that Dora should never have been given a gun. They were too readily available in her moments of despair.

In retrospect, after finding her earlier suicide note when she was thirty-one, I should have considered her vulnerability. Dora had thought of suicide before but could not bring herself to do anything about it. Had she owned a gun then, I am certain she would have used it because it is so easy. I'm sorry that her doctors did not treat her for depression. I also regret that I did not understand enough about her condition to say that she should not carry a gun. Her brother was intuitive enough to realize she should not have been a gun owner.

At one point Dora sold three of the weapons Rob gave her to raise money to move where he resided. She kept the one gun that she used to end her life. How many people exist today who should be evaluated for mental illness before owning a gun? Depression and mental illness are often hard to diagnose. I could not understand my own daughter 's condition, and how I wish now that I had been able to discern what was troubling her. I would have done so many things differently.

My younger daughter had a close friend whose brother visited his father in Los Angeles occasionally. On one trip, he was in the apartment of a girl he had become acquainted with. They were simply having a casual conversation when her boyfriend knocked on the door and became enraged that his girlfriend had another male visiting her. He left and returned with a gun and killed the young man. He took the life of a productive young man because he could not handle his own rage. I attended his funeral and listened to his distraught mother moaning, "Why? Why?" How futile such actions are! Many people could do with anger management before owning a gun.

I watched a responsible family member return from a government job, carefully unload his gun, and place it in a locked box high in a closet. That is what a gun owner with integrity does.

We need to consider carefully who should own a gun. We make strict laws about who can drive, but we are unable to curtail the ownership of guns by those who are a danger to themselves or to others.

Unfortunately, many ill people like my daughter remain undiagnosed. I believe she was bipolar and suffered from moderate personality disorder. I was not able to help her. A family member who met Dora for the first time expressed shock at her expression. She said to me, "She looks so angry." She had seen such a look before and recognized something I was too close to Dora to recognize. I could not see it, and her observations were not addressed. I have no doubt that the death of her beloved father so early in life contributed to her depression. I recognized that she exhibited what is called "a flat personality." She rarely showed any emotion but responded by simply shrugging her shoulders.

To those who would advise others to abandon their wayward children, I say no. How often people casually say that a parent is aiding and abetting a behavior. How glad I am that my daughter died loving and respecting me. I have only her cards and poems now saying how much she appreciated me. I would never change what I did. For years I supported and encouraged her to stand on her own. I did not abet but loved her. I cherish the times I took her to lunch or we shopped. I helped her plan her moves with the understanding that I would always be there for her. Please never abandon your children. Love them forever unconditionally. Then there are fewer regrets. I loved her to the end, my dear Dora.

My daughter never overcame the loss of her father when she was ten years old. The following is something she wrote about him:

To My Dear Dad with Love

It has been twenty-five years, and I think of you more than ever. You were the best dad a kid could have.

A birthday wish for you, that you are happy and content where you are right now. You are never forgotten and have a special place in my heart always. I can't wait until I see you again in the wonderful place we call heaven. You will meet the love of my life who loves

history like you do. I think I fell so deeply in love with him because he has so much heart like you and is a reminder of a great, wonderful man you are and always will be.

11
A Visit With Bret

Four years had elapsed since I last saw Bret, who was still living in the same care home. Our only
    contact had been by phone, and I had chosen a local phone number for my cell phone so he could call me without expense to his caretaker. Now, at last, I was flying west and would visit him and talk to his doctor,

whom I had contacted by email. My first stop was to attend the wedding of my step-granddaughter. There, my youngest brother joined me to help with the driving logistics. We rented a car, booked a hotel, and hoped to find Bret. As I feared, when we located Bret, he was drunk. Despite his condition, we had a productive visit with his local doctor, who spent some hours testing him. It was the doctor's opinion that Bret now needed more care than independent housing gave him. However, nothing came of this observation, which would take some legal steps to implement. Since his girlfriend had left, Bret had been moved to a makeshift room of his own built on one end of the outside patio. He seemed content with the arrangement since he always preferred to be away from people.

At the rear of the property was what appeared to be a chicken coop. I am sure I heard chickens. In the house, someone was preparing meals amid the ruckus of four small, barking dogs. Although Bret seemed thinner, he appeared to be getting enough to eat. I understood that a doctor visited weekly and prescribed medications, but the question remained: did the patients comply and take their meds?

Bret complained, as always, that he did not have enough money. Recent government cuts had been made, and the poorest among us suffered. He complained that he no longer received a bus pass, and the payee explained to me that the passes were cut because they were being sold for drugs or alcohol. It was my job to take him to a Walmart and purchase the shoes he always needed because of his constant walking. He admitted that he was panhandling for extra money, which obviously went for alcohol.

Although I was depressed with his arrangements, Bret expressed appreciation for a place to live. He had now spent ten years there, and the kind providers felt comfortable with him despite his drinking because, as they explained, "He is a good person and not dangerous." I have heard people wrongly and ignorantly assume that schizophrenia means a person is a potential killer. How wrong! Bret is gentle and caring. At times he expresses some intuitive understanding of others. I felt my mother also had possessed an uncanny ability to size up people, especially my father's associates who tried to use him. Bret had lost his father at age fourteen, and many times he had to fend for himself. He maintained his paper route and adapted to numerous situations without adult intervention. He also endured three years in the army with his mental condition and stood his ground. Living some years with me as a single mother had forced him to develop survivor skills. Perhaps that is why he is still alive despite his handicaps. As the eldest, Bret was never babied and was self-reliant against many odds.

Today Bret spends much of his time walking and is still a habitual early riser. He recently told me of a merchant who provides him with a spot in front of his business to panhandle in exchange for taking out his rubbish. Also a man came by and donated a coat and shoes to him. This breaks my heart, and I would never want his father to know this. But again, Bret has adapted as best he can with no help from family, friends, or society. I had urged him to join something like the Salvation Army, but Bret can't be around people. His condition prevents him from socializing.

For times when Bret feels uneasy with someone living near him, he has developed a way of protection by avoiding eye contact. He tends to mind his own business. When he recently became involved in a fight, he took responsibility for it and said it was his fault. Probably he was drunk. I worry constantly but know that there are no similar living options where I live. When I contacted the veterans hospital here, I was encouraged to leave him where he is.

Often I have lamented that I was not rich enough to care for Bret, but I knew of families with both money and political connections who had not been able to save their children. The law is stacked against such families and people like my son. Instead they reside in independent living facilities when the truth is they are totally unable to manage or save themselves. We once had "poor houses." My grandmother cried when her father died in such a place. For years, I have dreamed of a society where each town would have a place to care for those in need. I even named them Alvin houses after my children's father, who was kind and caring.

Bret had been in and out of VA facilities for alcoholism only to start drinking as soon as he exited the hospital. Perhaps follow-up could have helped, but he left on his own never to be checked on again. I have been able to email Bret's doctor for information since Bret has signed a paper allowing me to do so.

My new husband and I now live in a retirement home, and I know I could never again endure taking care of Bret. He quickly wears me down, so I do respect the untrained people who now have him in their home. I realize that little is accomplished on my visits, except that I can reassure him how much I love him. I have looked in vain for care facilities near me, but they do not exist. He calls me when he wants to, and I listen to the same complaints over and over. Now it is left to the kindhearted work of people, who are foreigners in our land, to care for him. Sometimes I wish I could outlive my son so I could properly bury him. I have a place paid for him beside his sister and Dad. I reminisce about the wonderful young boy we had who never made any trouble for us. One of his schoolteachers once commented on his "dry humor." It was only after the death of his father that I became aware of Bret's psychological problems. In spite of his illness, he has remained a good son, a sad and tragic son I could not help.

12

My Closet

To understand my family's illnesses better, I have opened my closet, where I recall a web of bizarre behaviors, a fabric of odd memories woven together in a strange design. Once, when an aunt and I were visiting a family acquaintance, I commented on my mother's nervousness. The friend was shocked that I would speak disparagingly of my mother. Immediately, my aunt confirmed my observation. She recalled a warning from her doctor about marrying into my mother's family, which the doctor described as very nervous. Mother was later given medication for panic disorder and obsessive-compulsive disorder.

As a child, I enjoyed looking through the family photo books. My mother's engagement picture was stunning: a three-quarter-length photo in which she was seated with one leg crossed, wearing a lovely, flapper-style lace dress. She had a cute turned-up nose and was a beauty in those days. Along with the photo, the long newspaper announcement caught my attention, and it helped me to understand where my mother was coming from. The article never mentioned that she had worked five years for a large insurance company. Instead, what caught my interest were the few words stating that my mother "was well known in religious and social circles." Mother had once commented that she was from a simple family. My father, however, had attended MIT and was a brilliant man. Reading the newspaper announcement, I began to understand my mother's life as a social climber. She spent most of her spare time as president of various organizations. Every time she acquired a new title, she had her picture in the local paper as president of another group. Whenever my parents moved to another town, Mother took little time to have her picture in the paper. The local pastors always found a willing organizer when they met Mother.

Suddenly I understood not only my mother but also her sister and my grandparents, who had moved to my large hometown from a rural town and sought to become noticed. Both my mother and her sister were beautiful and talented. They sang and played the piano while her sister also was an accomplished artist. Unlike their brothers, they had both completed high school, married well, and become involved in social organizations—church and clubs that brought them prominence.

When I young, I thought my parents looked like Myrna Loy and Clark Gable. They had a busy social life, and Mother's small closet was filled with lovely evening gowns that unfortunately were always too large for me. My brothers and I were aware of the photograph of a mystery woman in Dad's top drawer. When the woman was identified as the mother of our half brother and our parents settled into separate lives, we accepted the compromise they lived with. Finally I could see the fantasy life my mother strived for, which contributed to her nervousness and neglect of us. Her hours on the telephone running her social life, with a cigarette dropping ashes around her, was a burden she accepted just to attain social status.

I always considered my sister to be exceptionally intelligent, a teacher with several degrees. However, like me, she has never been able to shake the memories of our mother, which we constantly share from our closets. We often find ourselves relating identical experiences as odd memories are hung out to dry. My sister was born when I was fifteen, and I left home at seventeen; therefore, our lives were separate but remained intertwined with similar memories. While I recall a childhood filled with fun times, growing up with our three brothers, she missed that experience. My sister was always the baby, and we grew up separated by distance and experiences. I lived in California for years while she remained in the East. Not until the deaths of our parents did my sister begin to open up, to let things fall out of her closet. From her, I realized that I was not alone in suffering abuse from our mother and that I did not imagine my memories.

When our mother died, my sister and I divided the list of relatives to notify of the death. I called a cousin and an aunt, and oddly when I told them the news, they responded exactly the same. "She was a difficult woman," they exclaimed. "Yes," I said to my aunt, "and I had to live with her." Not only was my mother remembered as difficult but she also left a legacy of unhappy memories in many closets. Her father was self-centered, and Mother left three daughters-in-law divorced from my brothers and estranged from her. As I near the conclusion of my saga, I have had news of the premature passing of two cousins on my mother's side from addiction to alcohol and suicide with mental illness. A cousin called and related a brief message that was left on his phone concerning the death of his sister: "Diane died on the street of alcohol poisoning." No more details were given.

I continued to worry about the lack of care provided for my mentally ill son who is an alcoholic. These tragedies brought to mind the years I wished I knew my cousin Diane, who disconnected from the family when she married. Whenever I visited her mother, my aunt, she gave no explanations for her daughter's absence. I sensed how much my aunt missed her, but she made excuses for her, saying that Diane had been in car accidents and was hospitalized. My aunt said her daughter did show up unexpectedly from time to time. I realized how much my visits meant to her, particularly when I brought my own daughter and grandchildren. Once I placed my new grandson on my aunt's lap and took a picture of her smiling broadly. The table beside her was covered with medicine bottles that suggested how many physical problems she had. My aunt had been widowed at middle age and never remarried. Beside her bed were pictures of her dependable son and his wife's children. Strikingly, only an early portrait of Diane was displayed with none of her three children, who lived in another state.

I attended my aunt's funeral expecting to finally see my mysterious cousin Diane, but I was troubled to hear that she could not be located for her own mother's funeral. I heard a story of retirement in a motor home and that she and her husband could not be located. My cousin's untimely and tragic death from alcoholism reminds me that my own daughter, according to her diary, suffered from alcohol poisoning the week she died.

Many families have skeletons in their closets, but it is the extremes of addiction and illness in mine that are disconcerting. In contrast, many in our family have made us proud, including my two youngest children. They have become educated, been successful, served their country, and raised children. Among my relatives are two professors with doctorates and much talent. My concerns are with the genetic problems experienced by my eldest children and some relatives. I often wondered if the alcoholism could be traced as far back as my grandmother's father who died in the poor house. My uncle who spent time in mental hospitals was a quiet, gentle man, but under the puffs of smoke from his pipe, he hid his anger, I was told. My uncle and his brother were forced to leave school early to support the family, and this left deep scars with both men. My uncle lived a productive life, married, had children, and loved his job. Although he spent years in mental institutions, he lived to be ninety-three, still smoking his pipe. New medications had helped him. If only there was medication to help alcoholics now.

Like my mother, her father demanded attention incessantly. Each morning, when he got up, he took his vitamins and started exercising loudly with his dumbbells. No one else could sleep when he was awake. Grandma served his meals promptly three times a day. I will never forget how, in her late seventies, on her last day of life, she served his supper, sat on her bed with her apron on, and fell over dead. Whenever I visited them, Grandpa had greeted me at the door with a book in hand and started reading from his favorite religious passages. I would describe his personality as egocentric. This was a personality trait I saw repeated in three generations.

Similarly, I can remember Saturday mornings when I wanted to sleep but instead was rudely awakened by my mother who could be heard in the kitchen yodeling. She wanted everyone to get up when she did. Likewise, my sick son is inconsiderate and seeks attention. There are other instances of relatives who demand constant attention, so much so that I see it as a genetic disposition to being egocentric and immature. Sometimes Bret would go into the yard and make strange sounds like a wounded animal. Other times he made embarrassing remarks in front of company. This also reminded me of my mother, who frequently humiliated me in public by bringing up personal things. I remember having my new stockings and garter belt discussed in front of men. And when she bought me a razor to use in ballet school, she gave me instructions on using it in the taxi. I learned early not to tell her anything about my life or feelings because she broadcast everything.

In our closets, my sister and I found we shared a mystery: where did our clothes go? I was surprised when my sister related the same stories that had been perplexing me. Growing up, I remember certain favorite things in my closet. One summer I had horseback riding lessons and was proud of the riding outfit I wore. Following the lessons, the pants disappeared. Like so many items I enjoyed, I have no recall of giving them away or even outgrowing them. For my ballet performances, I had beautiful outfits made, such as the "Yellow Gal" costume sewn with colorful chiffon and a matching bonnet decorated with roses. Once I finished performing in an outfit, it was gone. I look back on so many personal things hanging neatly in the closet one day and gone the next. Where did my graduation dress go, my favorite coat, my Easter outfit, and even my toys? I didn't have my Shirley Temple doll or baby doll long when they suddenly disappeared. Did Mother take things and sell them, I wonder?

My sister and I affirm many similar experiences. We rarely had the pleasure of shopping for clothes. Instead we took what my mother brought home to us. We had few opportunities to make decisions or fill our closets ourselves. When I attended a prom, I rarely knew who my escort would be until I started down the stairs. Mother had always arranged my dates. Fortunately, they were good choices most of the time. I wish I had been a fly on the wall listening to her make the arrangements. When I became engaged at eighteen, it was not long before my mother concluded that my engagement was not suitable and went to my room, took the ring, and addressed it to my fiancé. She never did learn the correct facts about my boyfriend's background. If she had known, for example, that his father was a naval officer, she might have sung a different tune.

Along with the frequent articles Mother managed to have printed in the papers about herself were occasional news items she had printed about me without my knowledge. I recall one clip she sent in about me studying ballet in New York City. Unfortunately, she never consulted me, and the information was incorrect. She had evidently looked at a brochure of the school and selected one teacher among several that I was supposedly studying with. It happened that I never saw the man. Perhaps it was a trivial mistake, or possibly she could not pronounce the names of the Russian instructors I did study with and instead found a simple English name. I wasn't happy about the incorrect information. Later, when I married, she sent a notice to my hometown paper. Again,, she never asked for my permission, nor did she have any information. She selected the most inappropriate portrait, and the few lines of information were incorrect or missing. The information had nothing of interest. Throughout my life, I would find my picture in the paper with some incorrect copy because Mother had never taken the time to ask me anything. When I married, she sent notices to people she chose thinking they might respond with a gift. I found it all embarrassing.

Much more remains in the closet, but I only wish to point out the similarities that make me suspect the genetics of mental illness. My family has battled the illnesses of alcoholism, schizophrenia, and panic disorder, to name a few. In contrast, tucked away in the closet, we find artistic and musical talent, teachers, professors, and beautiful people. Our mother played the piano by ear and sang beautifully without ever practicing. Her father also was a natural pianist and early in his life played for silent movies. My mother and her sister, as mentioned, were gifted in many ways. I remember watching my mother get up on a stage and sing without ever warming up. Of course, she always sang the same song.

Our father was an inventor, a talented designer with two hundred patents to his name. I studied ballet and voice and love designing quilts. One of my brothers received royalties from a large company for his designs. My children have never expressed any artistic inclinations, but the two youngest have excelled in their professions—the military and teaching.

Without encouragement from our parents, I feel all of us missed our potential. During my father's constant absence from home, we meandered through life as best we could. My sister and brothers attended private schools while I graduated from public high school. During his high school years, my middle brother ran away and was located by my father in the military, under an assumed name, ready to be shipped to Korea. He returned home and received a football scholarship to an academy from which he graduated. My youngest brother left high school to marry. His last years at home with our mother and sister were contentious with the constant absence of our father. Later stories of my brothers' lives revealed that the youngest was sexually molested at private school by his headmaster, while at home he had screaming matches with our mother. Our mother's abuse of my middle brother devastated me for years and left my stomach in knots.

I imagine the potential we all might have had if we had been nurtured properly. What more could we have achieved? We all had talents that needed nurturing.

Is it a coincidence that some have been ill while others thrived? How is it possible that so many have not reached their potential or perhaps have been denied success because of abuse and neglect? I saw much talent in my brothers: the eldest was a choir soloist, talented at drawing, and had a wonderful broadcasting voice, which he used in Okinawa while in the service. I felt that with direction we all could have gone further. Unfortunately, our father was absent a lot in his later years, as he kept an apartment in New York City. At home, our mother destroyed us rather than encouraged us. It is amazing to me that the four eldest of us survive in our eighties while our younger sister has endured multiple illnesses. Both my sister and I contemplated suicide during our lives. Without the skeletons in our closet, and with guidance, how much more could we have achieved? Now we live despite the skeletons.

13

Skeletons

Memories often haunt me. Like skeletons, they return, stripped of identity, just pieces that I must struggle to understand. Trying to drown the past, some people choose to drink or take medications to survive. Others suppress the past, deny the existence of problems, and fail to learn from experiences. Some people drape themselves in religion and only live to earn a place in another life, while denying the opportunity to grow in the present. Life is not fair, and those who believe otherwise deceive themselves. I choose to learn from the past and embrace the future. I do not wish to wallow in the past but instead try to examine my life and learn lessons I can apply to the present. While I don't recommend dwelling on the past, I do hope to glean understanding from my experiences.

The street I grew up on as a child still holds many pleasant memories. Behind the walls, people lived and behaved in uniquely different ways. In our house, we were to be seen and not heard. Across the street at my girlfriend's house, I remember a large, vociferous family that conversed at each meal. The parents knew what assignments each child had prepared for that day. They helped with the tests and listened to their children's stories.

Throughout my childhood, we always had a girl attending secretarial school living with us. They took an interest in me and often took me home with them on vacations. One such trip was to Vermont in winter. I remember that I went with no suitcase or any kind of clothes at all. I recall crying when my unprotected knees turned cold. Fortunately, the girl who took me was small, so when we reached her home, I was able to wear her ski outfit and play in the snow. This experience remains vivid because it was an example of my lack of training on how to prepare for events of all kinds. Later in life I was impressed with a sister-in-law who had a talent for organization. I do not know where she developed this skill, but I realized that I was most unaware of what planning entailed. Throughout my life I suffered misgivings about my inability to prepare for anything. I recall getting on a train with thirteen dollars and no plans for several days of meals and sleeping with a child. This lack of foresight haunted me and made me feel inadequate.

Unfortunately, at my house, parenting was delegated. All three of my brothers and my sister were sent to boarding schools. No one inquired about classes I had selected for the semester. When I brought a report card home, it was left on a secretary by the door and was picked up and signed in the morning before I returned to school. I belonged to a group of girls, "the gang"—throughout my school years, and much of what I learned about life came from their conversations. Most of them had plans beyond high school, as their parents coached them on options for college and careers. I regret that neither the school nor my parents realistically prepared me for the future.

I sometimes wonder about the random early memories that remain with us. Of all the countless hours, days, and years of our childhood, I have a few vivid experiences that are constant in my mind. I recall being left independent a lot as a small child. One memory is of me sitting on my tricycle alone on a busy street, watching fire trucks put out a house fire. Another time I biked to a nearby dingle where I thought I saw an owl. My childhood consisted of numerous episodes in which I was far from home, alone, exploring the neighborhood with no one concerned about my whereabouts. I am not sure why certain incidents remain imbedded in my thoughts, but they are a constant. Another childhood memory is of me walking a block to kindergarten alone and immediately walking back home with a note saying that I had German measles. This was followed by confinement for several weeks.

When I was four, I recall playing with a neighbor boy named Bobby. I remember because he locked me in his rabbit cage and gave me raw asparagus to eat. Now who could forget that? Again this experience was never mentioned at home. Years later, when the same boy was set up as my date for a prom, I never said anything. After all, would he remember putting me in a cage?

My life consists of numerous times when I was alone or with friends without any accountability from home. As I grew older, I usually pocketed my bus fare and preferred to walk everywhere. Perhaps I felt I saw more this way, and it satisfied my curiosity. I recall walking to my grandmother's house and being attacked with punches by a stranger, a small boy. Of course, I never mentioned these experiences at home. My grandmother would say, "Boys will be boys," and leave it at that.

My brothers and I often went to a playground. One day some boys started throwing pieces of slate around, and one hit me in the knee, cutting it deeply. My brothers put me in our wagon that we had brought and pulled me on a long walk home. The incident remains in my memory because it was my father who met us and tenderly cleaned the wound. I could not forget this because the iodine hurt. It was my dad who always took over when I was in need and gently fixed my wounds. After healing, a large scar remained for most of my life. However, it was the tenderness of my father that remained in this memory of a deep cut. Looking back, it was always my father who appeared beside my bed when I cried out from a nightmare, and I had many. As gentle as Dad was in emergencies, there were times when he had little patience. I often ran down the stairs making a loud clatter, and once Dad appeared and scolded me for the noise I created. He made me go up and down twenty times. From then on, I slid down the banister when in a hurry.

When I was nineteen, my father planned a car trip across country for my mother, sister, and me. Since I had not yet learned to drive, he arranged for private driving lessons. I can't forget the first day of instruction because I scared the instructor no end. No one had ever sat me behind a wheel and explained things. I put my foot on the pedal and nearly ran through the red light near my house. You would think my father would have shown me something about the car. I did get my driver's license and shared the driving as far as Chicago, where we stayed with relatives. Luckily the rest of the trip was soon cancelled because Mother ended up in the hospital with severe pain, thought to be a kidney stone. I was relieved because I could not imagine driving across country and back with someone as nervous as my mother. I managed to drive us home with only one minor accident when I ran into the car in front of us at a light.

Following my graduation from high school, my father sent me to a private school in New York City. At the same time, I attended ballet classes at the American School of Ballet. During the first semester of ballet school, I began to have serious doubts about my ability at seventeen to become a dancer. First, I was too short. The director preferred tall, long-legged ballerinas. Secondly, I had only started serious training when I was seventeen compared to many who had studied for years. My prior experience had consisted of occasional small-town lessons by a local teacher with little ability in technique. Following one summer session of lessons in New York, I became her assistant teacher.

Following the close of the year at boarding school, I found myself unfocused. I later realized that the school was not accredited and that my experiences there had further contributed to my unrealistic preparation for life. My father envisioned no future for his daughter other than that of fame or a successful marriage. At the school I had rubbed elbows with some of the elite from southern society, who attended prior to having their coming-out debut at home. We had the pleasure of sitting in a private box at the Metropolitan Opera House throughout the season.

Another experience was attending a fraternity party where I was introduced to spiked drinks—with 50 percent gin, I was told afterward as I nearly collapsed. As a Yankee I learned about the Confederacy from the school owner, a southerner, who usually wore a Confederate sash about her figure and had portraits of General Lee on the walls.

After leaving finishing school, I wandered from job to job in an attempt to avoid returning home to my mother. While at the school, I had become involved with my French teacher's son. For me it was love at first sight, and we became an item. He and his mother were recent refugees from the ravages of World War II in France. Madame, my teacher, was a graduate of the Sorbonne while her son, Tom, had managed to survive Nazi extermination by jumping from a train headed to Germany. Soon afterward, he was captured and interred in a Nazi concentration camp, where he was eventually rescued when General Patton's troops entered France. Tom's education had been neglected during the war. Following allied victory, they moved to New York City and both found jobs.

At eighteen, I accepted an engagement ring from Tom against his mother's wishes and without any plans for immediate marriage. My parents quickly visited New York to pass judgment on Madame and Tom, and after an awkward meeting, I was taken home. I languished there for months with little contact with Tom. My mother eventually broke the engagement; she took the ring from my room, packaged and addressed it, and sent it back to Tom with no explanation.

I am sure that if my mother had known the facts about Tom and his mother, she would have accepted him and been on the phone gloating about the marriage. My parents never knew the true background of the family. Instead she mistakenly called him a foreigner. She wrongly believed that if I married him, I would lose my citizenship, which was not true. The fact was Tom had been born in a naval hospital in San Diego. His father was a retired naval officer. Madame's father had been a doctor, and she graduated from the Sorbonne. Mother would have had a field day boasting if she had let me talk. Instead my future happiness was never to be the same. Mother did not have the ability to seek facts but instead sat in a chair ruminating and fabricating the worst of possibilities.

Following a return to New York, I had uneventful jobs for several years, took voice lessons, picked up a new religion (my third), and routinely returned home to the farm, where my parents lived, to see my siblings. I recall bouts of depression and a lack of direction. Mother tried to interest me in going out with the milkman, but I thought I had lost the only love I knew in the Frenchman. I had long forgotten my aspirations to become a teacher.

During these years, my mother continued to upset me. Thoughts of suicide confronted me on two occasions. One time I grabbed the keys to the family car and headed down a mountain road to town, where I called a church counselor. I was spared at this time from driving over a cliff near the house. Some years earlier, I had contemplated jumping out of the second-story window but thought it might only injure me instead of ending my life. That day, I wrote in my dairy that I hated my mother, and typically she later read it. She always went through our rooms and read our mail. Opening our mail was a ritual for her. While one of my brothers was living at home, he received personal mail from the military, which he had just left. It was of a delicate matter, but she opened it anyway. After this happened several times, he told her that if she opened his mail again, he would leave. She opened his mail the following day, and he packed and left for good. She had learned nothing after opening our father's private mail and learning of his affair.

I knew that everything we told our mother was mulled over and twisted, and then her warped interpretation was shared with others. She wallowed in the pleasure of destroying our friendships and our lives. There was privacy for no one. To make it worse, when things she learned upset her, she got on the phone and sought sympathy. She was totally unable to think through a problem on her own but instead imagined the worst. She was obsessed by a need to disrobe everyone and claw over the skeletal remains.

Since my parents were obviously disappointed with my lack of success at becoming a ballerina, little was said about my future plans. I requested art lessons or even business school training, but both were dismissed. I was to have no more help. During periodic stays in New York City, on my own, I went to night school and learned to type—a lifetime, useful achievement. I would sometimes show up at a ballet school in an attempt to renew my passion for dance. But by then I realized that my parents had been given poor advice about how a ballet dancer is created.

They now seemed clueless about what to do with a daughter who was not appropriately married at twenty.

With a background devoid of conversation, I looked to adults I admired for direction. Among the friends I made in New York City were religious people who converted me to their cult. They had much influence on what I did for several years. This included the unexpected, brief return of Tom into my life. His mother refused to see me, so we had limited time together. I later learned that she died not long after we again broke up.

Following years of no direction, I eventually met a gentle, kind, but uneducated man whom I married with the encouragement of my religious friends. Prior to the wedding, my parents called me to the living room one evening. They had placed a single chair in the middle of the room where I was to sit while they lectured me on the follies of my future marriage. They warned me that my future would be filled with difficulties and financial hardship. They were correct, but the way they went about it was distressing. I've always thought that if they had sat me down at the kitchen table and had a friendly conversation over a cup of tea, I might well have changed my mind. Instead I felt like I was at an inquisition and burst into tears and ran to my room. I finally married only to have a life of my own, however modest. Having been thwarted so many times by my mother, I was happy to be independent.

I married with much trepidation. If anyone had expressed one word of doubt to me, I would have backed out. But all my friends were married, and I had no plans in motion for a single life. Once the date was set, I accepted the future with relief.

I chose the next Valentine's Day as our wedding date. No mention of a large wedding was ever expressed. My parents had moved to another state following my high school graduation, and I knew no one in the city where they now resided. Therefore, I selected a church in the town where my husband and I lived and had friends. It never occurred to me that I could have a large affair where my father would walk me down the aisle. Somehow, I sensed that a formal wedding with me as the center of attention, instead of my mother, would not be comfortable, therefore my wedding became a small family affair with my parents, grandparents, an aunt and uncle, my youngest brother, and my sister attending. At the time, it seemed like all I could wish for. Following the service, my father asked me if we had honeymoon plans. I was taken off guard for my husband and I had never discussed a honeymoon. Instead we returned to a sparsely furnished apartment where we had set up a few pieces of used furniture given to us by friends.

It is only decades later that I thought about what I had missed: the beautiful white dress and my father beside me as I walked down a church aisle with the sound of organ music accompanying me. In my elder years, I have often thought about buying a used wedding dress and having my portrait taken, white hair and all. Except for some shifts in body fat, I remain the same weight as when I married. I may still do it. It would be for me only, a remembrance of what might have been a special memory.

Later, following the wedding, I discovered that my mother had taken a recent photo of me and sent it to my hometown newspaper. Since she had never consulted me for information, the announcement was brief and devoid of any details about my husband or me. What upset me the most was the portrait she had chosen. It was by far the last one that I would have selected. It had been taken while I lived in New York City by a photographer I had recently met. I had worn a black party dress bought for my days at finishing school. I had worn my hair untypically on top of my head with a rose stuck behind one ear. Although I was pleased with the finished picture, it was not characteristic of my usual photos. It seemed too mature, too provocative in some way. Friends did not recognize me. Following the article in the local paper, my mother had to mention some derogative comments other people made about the picture. My former piano teacher was shocked. I was not only upset with the choice but also appalled that the article carried nothing about my husband or me. Mother had managed to humiliate me with her presumptive decision, and there was nothing I could do to change the fact. It was just another of her continuing attacks on my rights and emotions. She seemed victorious in her choices.

My girlfriends were all married before I was. The New Year's Eve wedding of one friend was a local event. Her father was president of the local college and a prominent pastor. I do not recall seeing the invitation, which my mother would have coveted. To my dismay, instead of attending the wedding with friends, I was put on a train back to New York for school, where I sat alone for two days until the other girls returned from the holidays. Meanwhile my parents attended the wedding together. As usual, I had no input in the decision. As I withered alone in my room at school, I never questioned what could have been. It was only when I began to look back that I evaluated the strange decision. Did my mother plan all of that so she could attend the social event in the company of my father without me? Did she see me as upstaging her? She had a history of thwarting my friendships. It was as though she wanted me isolated.

My first years of marriage were enjoyable. In time, we had four children and moved west, far from my mother, where I always had jobs when needed. Our lives were devastated by the eventual death of my husband from ALS, followed by a brief, difficult second marriage. Our move to the mountains then brought security and a marriage that lasted twenty years. In the third marriage, I was blessed to have a husband who saw to it that I completed the education I had started earlier when widowed. After my children grew and moved on, I was again faced with the illness and death of a spouse. Along with this, I began the lifetime struggle to care for my two mentally challenged children. My experiences with hitting bottom, fighting depression, and trying to help my family left me in a very different place. I began to challenge all that I knew—religion, my parents, education, and what I saw as the failure of society to help the needy. I dreamed of a place of refuge in every city in America where the challenged, the poor, and the lost could be helped. My late husband had envisioned a farm for the sick like Bret, where they could live and pursue productive activities, such as caring for animals. Often I dreamed of being a billionaire who could build some of these places, which I would call Calvin houses after my first husband, who was gentle and kind but simple. The ill and the lost would have a refuge from their problems and perhaps gain a sense of self-worth.

Somehow, through my maze of failures, I emerged with a sense of strength. For a year, I worked in a workroom for the intellectually challenged. I did not approve of the long hours they sat and worked at often-tedious jobs that benefited local businesses. I wanted them outside, taking care of animals or growing a garden. I wished they could take pride in a project. My ill son drove a truck for three years in the army, and he could still drive well under certain circumstances. Instead he was left to rot, to sit under the mulberry tree and drink his life away.

I recall with sadness the last visit I had with my mother. I had been a guest quilt artist at Dollywood in Tennessee, which I considered an honor. Following the show, my sister picked me up to take me to visit our mother. I vividly remember walking in the door of her apartment where she sat in a Victorian chair, glaring sternly at me. There were no greetings, no hugs, and no welcome. Instead she instructed my sister, "Go get the will." *Okay,* I thought, *I am not going to let this upset me.* I read it quickly and realized that since my father died, she had changed it completely. For some reason, she had given each of us five children different amounts of money, from two thousand for one up to forty-five thousand for another. I asked about the son who was left the smallest amount. "Does he know about this?" I questioned. "Yes," she replied, "he doesn't want my money." Nothing more was said, and I went on with plans my sister had made for me to take a trip to Charleston. However, in talking to the brother mentioned, I have learned that he has never gotten over the decision. I don't understand the motives but see it again as a form of manipulation and control. I advise against others ever treating their offspring so unjustly.

I wish that my early dreams of becoming a teacher had been addressed while in school and that I had learned more about management, parenting, and alternative work choices. I also want those who are limited in ability to be given an opportunity to be proud, even if it means being a paperboy like my son was or living on a farm, where my first husband grew up. I am fortunate to be able to write these memories, to empty my closet, and I hope others may find solace and direction in their life by reading the stories I have dragged out of my closet to scrutinize.

An essay my sister wrote and wished to contribute illustrates our similar experiences with Mother. She too experienced the vindictiveness of our mother and has written many pieces about their relationship. She did manage to have a large formal wedding in the town where she had spent some time growing up. Her husband's father was a successful doctor, and this fact impressed our mother. My sister walked down a church aisle in a borrowed dress, accompanied by our father. Mother, in a new outfit, sat in a front pew, gloating in the moment over her new relations with prominent people. My sister later wrote:

> Shopping with Mother was the most humiliating, demeaning, and embarrassing activity I ever had to endure. It was a nightmare! The only saving grace was that it only occurred once a year, and that was too often.

> Just prior to the shopping, she began to become more and more nervous and agitated. She, of course, took that out on me. By the time we got to the store, I was wishing I could disappear into the crowd and at least not appear as if I were with her or belonged to her in any way, shape, or form, though I was not with her in any way. I lagged behind her, head bowed and putting some distance between us. She once rudely bumped into a woman very hard and then turned on her with a greatly exaggerated tone as if she had been grievously injured and the victim of an unforgiving loss of etiquette. Once she hurled some demeaning comment as to the

woman's ethnicity, which I had no inkling how that could be related to my mother's rudeness. On Mother marched to the junior department. I was not included in the selection of any clothes. She moved from rack to rack, whipping and banging the hangers as she looked through the clothes. She muttered as she went through this process. She gathered some items together for me to try on and ordered me into the dressing room. On to the purchase counter where she became a different woman, with a radiant smile and a look of pride.

Why were my clothes for the year consisting of only three colors? They were red, blue, or green with matching knee socks. No jewelry or makeup was included. I was being dressed like a plain, old lady and in the least sexy clothes. At least it was over for another year.

14

Bret Missing

Weeks had passed since I was able to reach Bret by telephone. The caregivers at his home only answered during evening dinner hours. For the remainder of the day, there was a voice mail with an option to leave a message.

Then one day I tried again and found the telephone disconnected. Terrified that Bret might be alone on the street, I left messages with his doctor's office and then with his payee. The latter returned my call and gave me a number for the owner's home. Again I found only a disconnected number. After several days of calls to no avail, I decided I had to take a flight to seek answers. Amid my frustration, my younger son took control and booked a flight from Europe to California to see what he could find out.

We were soon advised that the phone number had been changed at the care home, and the owner had neglected to inform us. Meanwhile, my younger son found the owner at home and was advised of his brother's daily routine. Bret habitually left home at five in the morning and went to a shopping area where he panhandled until he had enough money to buy alcohol for the day. My younger son found his brother there and held out his hand to greet him. It took moments for Bret to recognize his well-dressed brother, who then offered to feed him. Following a breakfast, Bret left while his brother secretly trailed him in a car. Bret's daily routine was to leave his spot by the mall and walk to a liquor store when he had enough money to purchase vodka. He then went to his care home and drank to oblivion. Again and again his brother invited him to eat out, but Bret usually refused. When Bret was not available, he had discussions about his older brother's life with the owner of the care home. The conclusion he reached was that Bret was happy with his situation. He preferred his single room at the end of the patio rather than living upstairs in the house. The back door was always left open for him, and the several small noisy dogs alerted everyone when needed.

Our family decision was to try to get Bret to the VA hospital so he could get his VA card. My younger son learned that there might be more financial aid for Bret and that an evaluation of care would be made. This plan was explained to Bret, who agreed to be picked up the following day for the trip to the VA. His brother left him for his hotel, expecting to meet the next day. However, when he arrived at the agreed time, he was told that Bret had never come home the previous night.

I became concerned and decided to fly to California so I could join in a search. For three days, my son and I questioned shop owners and people who recognized Bret from a picture his brother had taken of him. We searched hospitals, the neighborhood, and any place we thought he could be hiding. The police were notified, along with his payee and doctor. The following days followed the same routine of driving and searching hospitals. Bret finally was listed as missing, and because of an earlier encounter with the authorities, he had a mug shot and fingerprints on file. Back at his room, Bret had left behind the new clothes his brother had bought him with the tags still on. And his Social Security card lay on his bed.

As time ran out for my younger son and me to stay, fear enveloped his caregiver and us. She related the story of a woman client who had been kidnapped and held in an adjacent town for three years. She was fed little and nearly blind when she managed to escape and return to the care home. It appears that some vulnerable people are mistreated and held for eventual benefits they might have. We were also told of a prank played on Bret two years earlier. He was driven miles to the border and left to find his way home by panhandling. I was never advised of this, along with other mishaps he experienced as a mentally challenged person.

Leaving without seeing Bret was devastating. We had done everything we could think of to find him. Some friends wondered if he was hiding because he was afraid to go to the VA. He had been treated there years earlier before I had a diagnosis for him. Did he feel he could not be without his liquor? He had no money, ID, or clothes when he left. His brother last trailed Bret headed for his home. We felt we could do nothing more but wait and hope he might return. However, as days passed with no word, we were left with foreboding fears of the unknown. Bret had been at the same home for ten years, and as much as we might find it lacking in our expectations of care, it remained a place where he felt content.

Before I traveled to search for Bret, my doctor prescribed medication to help steady my nerves. I have lived with concerns for Bret since he returned from the military. For forty years, my days have been filled with thoughts of how Bret might be doing. I had kept a home for him until I could no longer physically handle it. Leaving him at a care facility was the only option I had found. He had always refused to seek VA care, and I was forced to move on with my own life, a new marriage, and a move across the country.

As my younger son warned me, "Mom, we may never know what happened to him." I struggled to face each day with composure. I would wake and go to sleep with thoughts and misgivings about my decisions regarding Bret. Often I thought of all the world's mothers who had faced the same pain. Some days I thought of my childhood, of growing up during the war. Across the street from my house, a brave mother waited for news of her son during the Battle of the Bulge. Over four long years, other mothers in my neighborhood waited. On my street and the next one over, mothers were brought the terrible news that their sons were missing in action. These mothers lost their only sons and had to face life without a clue or a final hug.

Daily I wrestled with my worst fears: Is Bret being mistreated? Is he frightened? Is he trying to reach me? We knew that should he be found, his fingerprints would be in the system, and we would be notified. Other times I despaired over the system, which prevented us from getting him the proper care. The price of independence for Bret had been to destroy himself, preventing him from being acceptable in our company. I love him and cherish his childhood days. He never meant anyone harm, nor could he hurt another. But here we were despairing over his life.

The first thing I did when I returned home from looking for him was to take a lovely color photograph of Bret as a child, dressed in a shirt and pants to a store and have it framed. I hung it on my wall and told my husband, "This is the way I want to remember my darling, handsome, and funny son." I cannot think of the way he has deteriorated of late, the gray beard and the many missing teeth. I must cherish the childhood that he faced with courage, the loss of his father when Bret was fourteen, the many moves we had to make, and his proud military service. I see him taking care of himself with his paper route money and buying his own clothes. He raced on his motorcycle and struggled to finish high school.

When I lost his sister, Dora, I could not cry. I was in shock for months. I knew that she chose to die. As painful as it was, I did not wonder where she was or if she was hurt. But I worried about Bret every day because he was so ill and vulnerable. I wished to comfort him if I could.

My therapist pointed out that even if I found Bret and brought him home, I had no plan, no acceptable place to take him. Everyone said, "Not in my backyard." I couldn't subject my husband or my family to caring for him. He needed a public guardian, and I would have to get through the legal procedures to accomplish that. Life would never be the same for me, and I hoped to learn from my challenges enough to be of service and advocate for the mentally ill and homeless.

I couldn't find a nurturing place for my son that would protect him. Our government has closed the hospitals and left the mentally ill and vulnerable to live in the streets. I wish I could make a difference, but for Bret and me it may be too late. I have written as I see life, my life and my children's. I am thankful for the two successful children I do have.

After returning home without Bret, I started reading from Alcoholics Anonymous and began to understand what it means to be powerless to change those we love. I realized the necessity to care for myself and to survive for those who appreciated us. Two weeks after flying home, Bret was found by the police and returned to his care home, the place he liked and where he continued to drink.

Ten days later, I learned that Bret was again missing. As was his habit, he had left early in the morning to panhandle but had not returned. This time Bret remained missing for five months. Again we notified the police who saw only a pattern of disappearing, which caused them no alarm. It was my younger son's explanation of what might be happening that helped me to see some sense in this bizarre pattern. Bret was alcoholic, and he had mentioned blackouts to me. It remained a possibility that he could be having these spells and just continuing to walk to unknown destinations. What I had a problem understanding was why he did not ask for help. This remains an enigma to me.

Days became weeks, and weeks became months, and we had no clue about Bret's whereabouts. I feared the worst, and after some months, the toll of worry caused me to break out with shingles—not once but twice in several months. As before, the first thing I thought of each morning and the last thing at night was Bret. If only I knew. Again I thought of the mothers of missing sons during the war. How did they go on?

I decided to attend the National Convention on Mental Illness in Washington DC to take my stand for better mental health prevention. My younger son again reminded me that we might never find Bret, but we had to rely on the police assurance that without a body he could be alive. A missing person gives one no finality like death does. I had to force myself to live day in and out. My indomitable desire to laugh and be fun always prevented friends from realizing how devastated I was.

Then, after five months, I received a call:

"Mom, this is Bret."

"Where are you?" I cried.

"Mom, I am in a field in Lemon Grove with a girl I met. We have lived in a field across from a 7-Eleven for five months."

"Hang on," I begged, "while I get your provider on another line."

I was able to reach his caretaker who immediately got in her car and, within fifteen minutes, found him.

I couldn't imagine what condition Bret was in physically. With further questioning, I realized that he had been without water or personal hygiene for five months. He described sleeping on a tarp he found in the field at night and then panhandling for food during the day. "But," I implored, "you have SSI benefits and do not need to live like that." I also learned that Bret had been pursued and hit over the neck with an iron pipe, and he had bled so badly that he felt he would die. "Why, oh why?" I cried.

Bret was returned to his independent living home where they eventually had to shave his messed hair and long beard. What baffles me today is how people could live in our midst in squalor for months and never be stopped by the police. Again time has elapsed, and I have not been able to fly across country to see him. Always there is the lingering reality about what I can do if I do fly there. He has refused to get any ID, and I can't get him on an airplane and relocate him near me without some identification. We talked about the months in a field, and I can't grasp the indignity of living as he did. "Did you find a bathroom?" I had asked, and he explained that he defecated in the field and used paper towels to clean himself.

15

The Graveyard Revisited

Now, years later, the experience in the graveyard seems like a distant nightmare. I have learned to move on, and most importantly, I now accept my past and seek help for mental illness. My doctor was right when he diagnosed me with chronic depression. Looking at my life through the perspective of illness, I can now understand the feelings I had growing up—the loneliness, shyness, and fears. Flashbacks about my youth remain vivid, but today they have a different dimension. By nature I tend to want to laugh, to amuse others, to be entertaining. However, my memories of most of my interactions when young were tainted with an appalling need to escape. I can't remember a social experience in my past when I did not feel uncomfortable and fearful. All I could think about was getting back home to my room and privacy. Because of my mother, I had a social life; I was the nice little girl available to accompany the local boys to dances. Now I look back and wonder how these events could have continued because I recall saying nothing. Once I attended a weekend at a local university with a steady partner, and as memory serves me, I recall no conversation throughout the event. I danced with my partner throughout the visit but did not once speak to anyone. I was also his partner for three years of high school dances and recall no words between us as we jitterbugged through the events.

This was a part I played over and over. I had some wonderful dates—a doctor, a teacher, and boys I was attracted to—but I did not know how to talk to them. While I dated a young doctor, I never learned about his family, his plans for practice, or what he saw in me. What surprises me most is how long some young men dated me when I had nothing to say.

As I look back at the missed opportunities to be friends, I only recall the terrifying feelings I had of being unable to speak. The fact is I had no idea what to say, how to act, or what was expected of me. I was completely unprepared.

My school years were spent as part of a group of seven girls who walked to school together and always sat as a group during lunch. Mornings, we met at one girl's house, and loaded with our books and lunches, we hiked the half-hour trip to school. These walks were always accompanied by the stories of one girl who dominated the conversation through the years. Again I was left with no one to listen to me. Fifty years later I attended our class reunion, and there was a repeat of my one friend dominating the conversation. However, when she asked if we wanted to hear jokes, someone spoke up and said, "No thank you." By this time, with a college degree, I had learned to talk, and I no longer felt an inclination to hide or be quiet.

Throughout my school years, my girlfriends had prepared lunches, which I watched them consume with envy. I never brought a lunch but instead used the quarter my mother gave me to purchase something from the cafeteria. My money covered the choice of one item, my favorite: custard pudding. In hindsight I wonder why the girls never questioned why I brought no lunch. And why did I never consider making a lunch? It just never occurred to me. My mother never once suggested a bag lunch, nor did I know how to make one. In contrast, when I had children, I always rose early in the morning and made lunches. Still I can't explain why my childhood was void of this simple task.

In retrospect, we were not taught many simple tasks. Our beds were rarely changed, and we never learned to make them. Our clothes were left on the floor, and I do not recall how they got washed. In contrast, my children took their soiled garments to the laundry room and left them on the machine. I regret, however, that I was not organized and diligent about instructing my children to do many tasks. I had no experiences to fall back on.

This inability to express myself determined the future I chose with my first husband, who like me was inexperienced and shy. Unlike him, however, I eventually broke out of my cocoon and became a butterfly. I attribute my immersion into a normal social realm to my opportunity to go to college. No longer devastated and hurt by my mother's criticism, I relished the opportunity to express my opinions at college. I remember my first day in college with a thrill. It was a class on Childhood Growth and Development. I could have pinched myself with excitement at the realization that I was sitting in a college class. What followed was an opportunity to speak and be heard, which I never thought I would know. My advisor thought I had a great curiosity, and she encouraged my pursuit of an education. College enabled me for the first time in my life to be heard and valued. My family never commended me on my college experience. A sister-in-law asked me, "What are you going to do with that?" She saw no future in going to college unless it contained job preparation. I should have answered her by saying, "I only want to be intelligent and informed. I am tired of being ignorant."

My advanced education came late in life, but it gave me an opportunity to confront my past and face a difficult future. My third husband also seemed to appreciate my natural curiosity, and he enabled me to complete my degrees.

Coming out of my burrow of depression enabled me to confront life free of much of the illness I suffered. No longer did I feel uncomfortable with people, but rather I learned to engage them. I recall a conversation with my father once when he said, "The problem with being educated is that it is hard to find people to talk to." My feeling is that being educated should allow one to discover the hidden nuggets of what others are thinking. My father liked to sit in a bar in New York City and observe others. I believe the value of knowledge is to interact with others. I had spent my life as a fly on a wall, looking fearfully at the world instead of reaching out. Although I learned to immerge from a scary place, I still required medication for depression. This helped me to move more easily in social spheres. I have survived the devastation from abuse and the tragedies I encountered in life partly because of an attitude of hope and optimism. I found that the finality of death, which I encountered with my daughter, taught me to accept that she was gone and free. I was the victim who had to face the challenges of loss and learn to live. I could have collapsed in the cemetery and given up, but I somehow moved on. Having two wonderful, successful children following my first two offspring gave me the motivation to hang in there and live.

Often," I wonder how my life might have been altered if I had been given opportunities to express my feelings about abuse and depression. I wish that while in school we had been given the chance to talk about our home life. Imagine what might have become of a child being diagnosed early with depression because he or she had the opportunity to share his feelings in school. The school let me down as did my family. If only I had been diagnosed with mental illness while in school. All that one had to do was to ask questions. I wish I had been able to talk about my home life. My mother was very ill, destructive, and unkind. If only someone had recognized the problems she created for her family. My father withdrew from us and had a separate life, which left us all hanging on a limb in confusion. A child should be prepared for life in many aspects, which some feel a family should handle, but my family was negligent. My siblings and I were kept in silence and humiliated by criticism. Mental illness was the final blow to me, and I never understood it until it was almost too late. I wonder if I could have protected my daughter if I had been able to understand myself. I realized too late that I lacked many skills as a mother because of my own upbringing.

How many of us wish that we could live life over, or that we had known then what we know now? Life does not give us that opportunity, and we can only learn from our mistakes. All I can do now is share my experiences in the hope that others may benefit from my mistakes. I still do not have answers to caring for the mentally ill. My son is in limbo. I fret daily that I cannot help him. I have had to save myself because when I am with him, I overreact to the problems he creates that remind me of my mother. He always knows how to upset and annoy me. He persists in dredging up the past and the crumbs I wish to forget. I am unable to communicate with him. He needs someone to help him, but I am not that person.

Since I now live in a retirement home with my fourth husband, I cannot bring Bret home even to visit. Daily I hope that today I might find a place for Bret near me. Always I have a lingering hope that the VA will step up and place Bret in a secure environment. As the reality of aging encompasses me, I keep a lingering hope that I may see Bret cared for properly before my life ends. Against my younger children's advice, I still hope to make the flight to San Diego from Myrtle Beach for a last visit with Bret. We all know the scenario that will occur. I will drive up to the care home where Bret will have been cleaned up in anticipation of my visit. Inevitably he will be drunk and refuse to go to lunch with me. "Mom," he will beg, "do you have a dollar?" I know this scenario by heart. I will still love him and wish against all odds that I could protect him. All of this may never play out again, but I am left with the hope that I will somehow pull myself together, book a flight, and embrace my son, my first child, born on Friday the thirteenth.

APPENDICES

Appendix 1: Newspaper Article

While living in a small town, I had the opportunity to be interviewed for an article about my son's mental illness. The following has been slightly edited to make it more concise:

> Anne's son is disabled. It's not a handicap you can readily see. Bret isn't blind. He doesn't need a wheelchair. He's schizophrenic.
>
> Some people might call him "crazy" or "nuts" or even "not all there." Anne calls him her son and she loves him, although she doesn't know what to do with him.
>
> "There is so little known about mental illness or about the way it should be treated. There are medications, but I can't force my son to take them. It's almost impossible to know what to do.
>
> "He was a handsome baby and a lovely child. Everyone told me what a wonderful boy he was. Growing up, he had a paper route, graduated from high school, worked a year and then went into the army for three years. I didn't know there were any problems at all."
>
> "It was six years ago, when he came out of the army, that I began wondering about my son. Now, six years later, he has never had a job.

"At first, I thought my son was just an alcoholic. He had two accidents. both related to alcohol abuse. I tried to get him to go to AA, but it never worked for him. I was told that I would have to let him hit bottom first before he would accept help.

"I tried everything. He was asked to leave our house many times. When I discovered him sleeping in the park in the rain, I had to help him.

"Finally, it was suggested that I have him tested. After a month, he was diagnosed with schizophrenia, and in addition, his IQ was low. I was told that he probably would never work, get married, or have a normal life.

"Mental illness is more common than most people realize. About 15% of the population suffers from some form of mental health problems. It's amazing, when I tell people about my situation, how many relate a similar situation in their family. However not all families are open to talking about the skeletons in their family closet. People often hide mental illness or are ashamed to discuss it."

"Personally, I don't know which was harder, saying my son is an alcoholic or that he has what is called a dual diagnosis, that is alcoholic and mentally ill. Many parents don't realize that they can get financial help through Social Security. It provides a small portion of my son's living costs.

"Housing is a huge problem. I had to buy a house to keep my son in since I could not have him live in mine. This led to great financial disaster for me. If his IQ were lower, he would qualify for another program and have housing furnished. But for now, it is up to me to supply housing for Bret.

'I feel that society is negligent about caring for the ill. All society is doing now is paying for him to hide and vegetate. We continue to refuse to spend money to house the mentally ill."

Appendix 2: To Whom It May Concern

Following a meeting about Bret in the office of a local judge, I tried to implement her directions. The following is a letter I wrote to her concerning my inability to follow her recommendations. I felt that I was being sent in a continual circle where I received no help for Bret.

At the request of the Public Defender, I have taken Bret to the local Alcohol and Treatment Center where we talked to someone in charge. He referred Bret to a halfway house.

I had an appointment on August 9 for Bret when he was evaluated by a nurse and found not appropriate. We were referred to the local hospital alcohol treatment. There we were seen by another nurse. Bret was also seen as inappropriate there. I then talked to a doctor and an administrator, and it was again felt that Bret was not clinically appropriate for their facility. I was asked to get a list of nursing facilities for long-term care for Bret from Mental Health. They said they have no lists. I was referred back to the first interviewer for help.

Everyone I talked to feels that a conservatorship would best serve the interests of Bret. They recommend a court-ordered conservatorship where he is required to seek treatment. However, I have been informed that there are no psychiatrists available locally for this procedure.

A locked facility in another city was mentioned. However, I ran out of energy and options to pursue help. I purchased a home to house him where he remained for eighteen years. I understand that for me to become a conservator could lead to my being held responsible or even sued.

Appendix 3: Dora's Poems

Have faith in what you
Believe and don't give
Up on your dreams.
Do what you feel is best for
Your well-being. You can do it!

Dora's Prayer

I am a strong person, and I will
Prevail. God, Jesus Christ, my
Lord, and my father who passed
Away are with me, giving me
Their strength to carry on.
Take it minute by minute. You
Are just fine. Have faith.

Life

Life, how I ponder you.
How did you come to be?
Like me,
You are so perplexing.
I can't figure you out.
You bring such happiness,
Then you give such sadness.
You bring love.
Love, the strangest emotion:
It can be so wonderful
When it's good.
Love is so powerful when
You have it and nurture it.
Life and love!
Like they say, life goes on and so do I.

Goodbye

"94" should be a very interesting
Year. It's either going to be
The worst year of my life or the best. I
Hope for my sake it's the best. Otherwise,
I'm kissing my life goodbye.

No More Pain

I pray and hope it never comes
To this. If it does, I'm extremely
Sorry if I hurt anyone. Please forgive me if
I died in vain. I have been hurt too
Many times in my life.
My heart has been literally
Ripped to shreds. Life has
Taken its toll on me. I love you all.

Appendix 5: Essays

These two essays, written by my sister, seem appropriate to include, as they touch on the emotional feelings we both suffer from.

Will you always be there, Mother? Will the memories and especially the effects of growing up with you forever linger? I've tried so long to learn a different path. It is so hard. It takes my constant thought and drains and saps me of mental strength.

In eighth grade, I was walking to school one morning, and suddenly I began to disappear. Rationally I know that you think this could not happen, but it was happening to me. My mind and entire being were being drawn totally and irrevocably into the large tree beside me. I was being absorbed by it and was powerless to stop it. I was frightened as if I were falling to my death over a precipice, desperately trying to find a small branch, anything to cling to. Then, slowly, I was released by the power in the tree, but would it happen again? What had happened? I continued to school being careful not to step on a line so that I would not break my mother's back.

Mother never let me in the kitchen except for a few times to watch her boil fudge or roll out a piecrust. I knew nothing of any practical nature when I married. I was afraid and empty. I shall never forget that shortly after I was married, I asked a neighbor how long to keep a sponge that is used to clean in the kitchen. I didn't know how to hang up wash or fold sheets. This is not good for self-esteem. It made me determined that my children would know the practicalities of life when they went on their own. I also haunted the library and read books on how to care for a household. But, to this day, it is difficult for me to have any friends. Actually, I have none. I stand back clueless and afraid with a protective wall about me.

A footnote about my sister: After graduating from private school, she attended a university and received a teaching credential. It seems incredible, but on graduation day, she walked alone down the aisle to get her diploma with no one in the audience to congratulate her. I was living in California at the time and had given up trying to correspond with my sister because of our mother's intervention. My sister later married, had four children, and received several more degrees. She taught and supported her family for twenty-three years. Life has been difficult for her emotionally and health-wise. I applaud her courage and persistence in the face of overwhelming odds. Whether it is abuse, cancer, stroke, or other problems, she keeps laughing.

REVIEWS

Family Skeletons: A Web of Mental Illness is one woman's account of dealing with mental illness and alcoholism in her family. She shares her struggles dealing with grief following the suicide of her mentally ill daughter. She writes a compelling account of her efforts to work with social services and mental health agencies to find help for her son who suffers from schizophrenia and alcoholism. It is an account of one woman's love and persistence. Her story serves as a testimony to others.
—Susan J. Olson, MD, psychiatrist (SJO/tk 00023984)

If you want to read a poignant, realistic account of a daughter, wife, and mother's struggles against seemingly insurmountable odds in life and her survival, this is your read. If you care about lost, ignored, sick souls, this is your read. After tragedy upon tragedy, she survived to share her story.

—Louise Greene, teacher.

BOOK BLURB

Journal of a widow's challenges raising four children, two with mental illnesses. Accounts of her childhood in a dysfunctional family with discoveries of genetic alcoholism and personality problems.

ABOUT THE AUTHOR

At forty, I was a widow raising four children and a first-time college student, contemplating a third marriage and facing my two eldest children's diagnosis of mental illness. I began to confront my memories of childhood in a dysfunctional family and discovered family secrets with a genetic disposition toward alcoholism and personality disorders. I married for a fourth time but had to let go of my schizophrenic son. My story is for all who face unexpected challenges in life. This is my family story, skeletons from my closet.

Printed in the United States
By Bookmasters